Praise for
I Thought This Would
Make Me Happy

With candid illustrations, biblical insights, and practical takeaways and action steps in every chapter, *I Thought This Would Make Me Happy* is the positive change agent every relationship needs. Ditch selfish expectations, embrace genuine joy, and settle for more in your marriage!

Jodie Berndt, bestselling author,
Praying the Scriptures for Your Marriage

None of us set out to be unhappily married. Chelsea Damon cuts to the heart of our marital issues, which, in truth, are the issues that plague every human heart: selfishness, pride, and anger. Chelsea points to a better way of living and loving—God's way. This book is the soul surgery we all need—both in marriage and in life!

Joanna Weaver, bestselling author, *Having a Mary Heart in a Martha World* and *Embracing Trust*

I Thought This Would Make Me Happy is like finding a kaleidoscope of marriage advice. With each turn of the page, I see renewed beauty in God's purpose for it. Chelsea Damon breaks down lofty (and often distorted) concepts about marriage and teaches us something new. This book will change you and your relationship if you implement the actionable steps inside.

Ciara Laine Myers, author, *Glasses Off: Seeing God When Your Vision Is Gone*

T0198280

Whether your wedding was last century or last week, marriage is hard. Blending the personalities, habits, and hang-ups of two distinct people can often be an invitation to conflict and even chaos. Thankfully, Chelsea Damon has crafted a marriage manual that will empower you to weave understanding, forgiveness, and intimacy into your relationship with your spouse. The practical advice and biblical guidance in this book will encourage effective communication and help you cultivate true joy as you build a marriage that reflects the gospel to a watching world.

Karen Ehman, *New York Times* bestselling author, *Keep Showing Up: How to Stay Crazy in Love When Your Love Drives You Crazy*

I THOUGHT THIS WOULD MAKE ME HAPPY

I THOUGHT THIS WOULD MAKE ME HAPPY

HOW TO FIGHT LESS, FORGIVE FASTER, AND CULTIVATE JOY IN YOUR MARRIAGE

CHELSEA DAMON

ZONDERVAN
BOOKS

ZONDERVAN BOOKS

I Thought This Would Make Me Happy
Copyright © 2024 by Chelsea Damon

Published in Grand Rapids, Michigan, by Zondervan. Zondervan is a registered trademark of The Zondervan Corporation, L.L.C., a wholly owned subsidiary of HarperCollins Christian Publishing, Inc.

Requests for information should be addressed to customercare@harpercollins.com.

Zondervan titles may be purchased in bulk for educational, business, fundraising, or sales promotional use. For information, please email SpecialMarkets@Zondervan.com.

ISBN 978-0-310-36779-6 (audio)

Library of Congress Cataloging-in-Publication Data

Names: Damon, Chelsea, 1991- author.
Title: I thought this would make me happy : how to fight less, forgive faster, and cultivate joy in your marriage / Chelsea Damon.
Description: Grand Rapids, Michigan : Zondervan Books, [2024]
Identifiers: LCCN 2023051536 (print) | LCCN 2023051537 (ebook) | ISBN 9780310367772 (trade paperback) | ISBN 9780310367789 (ebook)
Subjects: LCSH: Marriage—Religious aspects—Christianity. | Communication in marriage—Religious aspects—Christianity. | Interpersonal communication—Religious aspects—Christianity. | Happiness—Religious aspects—Christianity. | BISAC: RELIGION / Christian Living / Love & Marriage | RELIGION / Christian Living / Spiritual Growth
Classification: LCC BL462 .D366 2024 (print) | LCC BL462 (ebook) | DDC 248.8/44—dc23/eng/20240209
LC record available at https://lccn.loc.gov/2023051536
LC ebook record available at https://lccn.loc.gov/2023051537

The author is represented by Alive Literary Agency, www.aliveliterary.com.

Cover illustrations: Adobe Stock / Getty Images / iStock
Interior design: Denise Froehlich

Printed in the United States of America

24 25 26 27 28 LBC 5 4 3 2 1

To my mother, Susan,
who has never stopped praying
for me, my husband, and our children.

Contents

An Invitation to Change

When I was a kid in church, it was common for youth leaders to encourage adolescent girls to write down a list of everything they wanted in a husband. I think the idea behind the list was to get us to think about the traits we wanted in a partner so we wouldn't settle for anything less than our clearly defined list of deal-breakers. This was my first list:

- Loves Jesus
- Wants six kids
- Knows how to cook
- Is kind

Well, my list changed quite a lot over the years. Especially the number of kids I wanted. At one point, my list took up an entire page, and I prayed over it in faith, knowing God would love nothing more than to introduce me to my tailor-made man at the perfect (very soon) time.

Fast-forward to my first date with Josh, drinking coffee way too late at night at a café a stone's throw from our college campus. At that moment, *he* was my list. Everything he was that wasn't on my list was now officially added. Everything he lacked that the list previously called for were now nice-to-haves but not deal-breakers. I knew he had his quirks, but if he had even a few of my nonnegotiables—"loves Jesus, is kind, is hardworking"—I was confident the rest of the list would work itself out.

Fast-forward once more to the present day. It *has* worked out! Josh and I recently celebrated eleven years of marriage, and we're consistently happier now than at any other time in our relationship. It's truly a wonderful feeling. But it took a lot of work, and many couples just like us never get this far. In fact, it's fairly *uncommon* for a couple to make it to ten years or more, let alone be happy. Statistics show that divorce rates are at their highest between five and eight years of marriage.

Maybe just this morning you caught yourself wondering, *What happened? He checked all my boxes. Why is there no joy, no friendship in our marriage? I thought this would make me happy.*

If that's how you're currently feeling about your relationship, I have good news and bad news. The good news is that almost every couple feels this way at one point or another in their relationship, which means you're far from alone. The bad news? Your relationship isn't going to get better on its own. In fact, it will likely get worse—that is, unless you decide to initiate change.

You may be thinking, *Why am I the one who needs to make this change? I'm not the source of most of our problems.* Even if that were true, you picked up this book because you're concerned about your marriage. You took your mental binoculars and looked down the path you're on and you don't like where you're headed. Which means both you and your spouse will need to change if you want your marriage to change. And when you recognize what needs to change and then take action, you will have stepped off your current path and onto one that has a much brighter future.

Christ designed marriage to be a picture of his unwavering love for us. And yes, at times we make it a very imperfect picture, like an old dusty portrait you might find hidden in the junk bin at an antique shop. But through grace and perseverance, your marriage can overcome both your own and your spouse's faults, as well as the trials you're walking through. Your relationship can be rescued from the bin, dusted off, and polished, so that once again its original design and purpose can be unveiled.

Today, Josh and I can *feel* the difference in our marriage. And I want you to know that you and your spouse can get there too. Yes, it *is* possible. It wasn't easy for us, and I can't promise it will be easy for you. But I do know it is so worth it. As you read through the pages that follow, I pray that God will give you and your spouse hearts like soft soil, ready to receive his word. And I pray that what grows from your willingness to initiate change is a deeply rooted and vibrant marriage that, like a sunflower that turns toward the sun, continuously points back to Christ. A renewed and life-giving marriage is indeed possible, and I invite you to take the first steps toward change.

PART 1

WEEDING AND SEEDING

For change to occur in a marriage, we need to do some weeding and seeding—in our own lives and in our relationship. These tasks require taking a hard look to see what has been growing while we haven't been paying attention. Some good and productive things may emerge, such as camaraderie, tenderness, and trust. But alongside those good things may come some undesirable things, such as resentment, pride, and selfishness. Once we see what we've allowed to grow, we can weed out what we don't want and cultivate what we do want in our marriage—new, unifying traits based on grace, unity, and joy.

Weeding out what we don't want requires taking a step back from any destructive patterns and humbling ourselves before God. When we do violate God's will, we must approach him with a heart of repentance. It's also important to acknowledge that we are no better than our spouse in the eyes of God—that we are both broken people in need of forgiveness. This realization requires humility, transparency, and the willingness to admit we have wronged our spouse and God.

Imagine the positive change that can result from freely allowing God to speak into our lives, to correct us, and to provide us with wisdom on how to restore our marriages. If this were our default response when things become difficult, our marriages would undoubtedly improve. Unfortunately, our default response tends to be a quick reaction to whatever our spouses did and a prideful assumption that anything we did is clearly a legitimate response to their actions. Or we may default to avoidance, trying to keep the peace by refusing to confront the concerns we have with our spouses or minimizing the concerns our spouses have with us.

How much better would it be if our go-to response were to ask God for guidance, respond in love, and do what is right, no matter how we feel in the moment? This requires prioritizing our obedience to God over our emotions, which in turn requires maturity and self-discipline. It also requires having an others-centered mentality, as exemplified in the life of Christ. Instead of condemning us for our failures and mistakes, he chose to love us and die for us, making the ultimate sacrifice so we could have fellowship with him and the Father.

We can set this example for our spouses, making the sacrifice to be obedient to the Father, to love our spouses with our words and actions, and to enjoy a deep friendship that embodies what marriage is meant to be. Ultimately, when we seek the face of God, align our hearts with his, and willingly approach our spouses with wisdom, grace, and love, we create a relational atmosphere in which the peace and unity we long for can become a joyful reality.

As you read through the chapters in part 1, I invite you to look at your own heart with eyes wide open—to put on X-ray glasses and peer into the motives, values, and fears that drive your actions and reactions. We'll look at how sin can creep into our lives through idolatry, selfishness, pride, and anger, and how these issues affect our own hearts as well as our day-to-day relationship with our spouses. We'll consider the surface symptoms of sin that often appear in marriage and look into the deeper reasons those behaviors exist, how they're destructive, and how we can mitigate them in the future.

Before diving in, ask God to humble your heart and help you see yourself the way he sees you—with naked honesty yet unrelenting love. Even if it seems like everything that's wrong with your marriage is your spouse's fault, I encourage you to set that thought aside for now. The goal is not to learn how to better identify sin in your spouse's life but to work first on your own heart. By seeking repentance for sin and drawing closer to Christ, you do the weeding and seeding necessary for building a redemptive relationship with your spouse.

CHAPTER 1

Know Your Treasure

s I was growing up, there was never a time when I didn't have a person—one relationship I relied on for a sense of security and identity. When I was little, it was my twin brother. We did everything together—school, birthday parties, and even sleeping in the same bed. When I was older, my person was a best friend, and we typically spent every weekend hanging out together. Around the same time, boyfriends entered the picture. And if a boyfriend and I broke up, I ran right back to my best friend and picked up where we had left off.

The idea of *not* having that one person, someone who would fully accept me no matter what, was unfathomable. It was terrifying to even consider the idea of being on my own without, at the very least, someone to text, "Good night."

As you might imagine, this relational dynamic made the prospect of marriage extremely desirable to me. I loved the idea of being wholly joined to someone who would not only never leave me but would never want to. Someone who not only knew my flaws but accepted them—or maybe even thought they were cute.

For years, I dreamed about the day my person and I would be locked in love and taking on the world together. And eventually, that day came. Josh and I stood before a small gathering of friends and family on one of the only sandy beaches in Washington State and said our vows while we shivered in the wind.

Fast-forward fifteen months, and we were both still in college, caring for a baby, working jobs that barely enabled us make ends meet, and trying to make life work. That's when I began to question why things didn't feel right. I had found my person; we'd said our vows; and we really did love each other. *Why was our relationship so hard? Why didn't we feel like a team? What was missing?*

I had been wrestling with these questions for months when I finally reached a turning point. I was standing alone in the kitchen one night and Josh was in the bedroom. We'd just had another argument about the little money we had—specifically, about the difference between what was reasonable to spend and what was splurging. At the time, buying a bag of corn chips was splurging. To avoid a fight, I'd sometimes buy a new bag of chips while he was at work and stash it somewhere so I could just refill the old bag. Desperate times call for desperate measures.

Josh was stressed, and his stress showed up mostly in lectures about spending, which turned into arguments each time I came home from Kroger with more than three bags in the trunk of our car. But we both knew it was more than that.

We'd gotten pregnant with our son just six months after we said our vows. Being the type who typically has a "things will work out" mindset, I was excited to bring a chubby-cheeked combination of me and Josh into the world. But I stifled that excitement when I felt Josh's overwhelm seeping out of his body like a cold sweat, which was often.

I never blamed him for feeling that way. It's not that he didn't want kids, but he hadn't thought he would become a parent supporting a family of three just over a year into our marriage.

That night as our baby slept and Josh got ready for bed, I stood in the dark kitchen, feet stuck to the cold tile floor, feeling really alone. It was in the quiet of that heart-sinking evening that I made a decision. No more manipulating my circumstances. No more leaning on other people to make my life what I wanted it to be. None of that ever helped anyway.

I realized I could no longer pressure Josh to be everything I needed. To fill my insecurities. To protect me and keep me from ever needing to venture out of my comfort zone—something I'd done with all my best friends and boyfriends up until that point. Josh and I were still a team, but as far as my unhealthy dependence on him was concerned, the pressure was off.

"It's just you and me now," I said to God while holding my arms at the elbows and staring up at the kitchen cabinets. "I don't really know what this will look like, but I'm going to start by simply being content with having you. I don't need to fill my life with people and things to feel safe and loved. Being with you is more than enough."

I felt God's gentle presence saying, "Good. Let's try this my way now. I know you'll see the difference." And in that moment, I felt free and light, like a weight had been lifted from my shoulders. I knew this was what God had always wanted for me, and now, perhaps for the first time, I wasn't fighting anymore. I was no longer saying, *Yes, God is everything,* while anxiously working behind the scenes to make sure the people I love would never leave, my future looked secure, and I'd never have to be alone.

It was a turning point, but it didn't mean my struggle was over. In fact, it was just the beginning of a long journey of learning to depend on God. And yet, rather than dreading it, I was excited. This surprised me because the idea of giving my plans and hopes to God with an open hand was still a scary one. *What if the future he wants for me doesn't include the things I have always wanted for myself? What does receiving my fulfillment from Christ instead of expecting to be fulfilled by others even look like?*

Everything felt unknown and uncertain because I was surrendering my right to manipulate relationships and circumstances to get what I wanted. And I knew that making changes in my real, everyday life, would take a lot of humility and practice. But I hoped that by allowing myself to enjoy Christ—to treasure him above all else—I would also learn to find joy in so many of the things and people over whom I had no control. My husband being one of them.

At the time, many of my friends were in the same boat I had been in before I married Josh, looking for that one person or one thing that would finally fulfill them. Some went through multiple relationships, thinking each person was exactly what they were looking for until, after a short while, the illusion started to fade and they realized they hadn't found their person after all. What they once thought was their treasure suddenly turned into a frustrating obstacle or detour. Then they felt the added anxiety of worrying that their quest for happiness and fulfillment was ticking away faster than it had been the day before.

So they began to date almost in panic mode, trying to find their person before it was too late.

But what if, like me, you found your person a while ago and you're starting to realize (or maybe you realized a long time ago) that they haven't—and can't—make you happy and fulfilled in the ways you hoped? What do you do then?

Some decide to accept their fate, settling into a roommate routine in which they do just enough to live harmoniously with their spouse. These folks wouldn't call their marriage enjoyable, but it's not a bad place to coast either. They don't fight much with their spouse, but they don't laugh much with them either. Others decide to take every opportunity to change their spouse and their situation. Obsessed with their own discontentment, they nag and berate. They embitter themselves toward their spouse, focusing on their disappointment about who their spouse is (or is not) and what their spouse does (or does not do) for them. In a frantic attempt to get what they want, they confront and criticize, believing that what they hope for will only come about by force.

If you can relate to either of these scenarios, or perhaps to both, you may need to ask yourself the same question I had to ask myself: *Have I been looking for my treasure in all the wrong places?*

That night in the kitchen, I finally acknowledged that Josh wasn't supposed to be my treasure. He was a lot of wonderful things—generous, kind, smart, hardworking, and handsome— and for years, I searched for a treasure that looked just like that. But what I didn't realize was that there was a treasure far greater than a handsome man coming home to me at six o'clock each evening. An eternal treasure that would never fade, never lose its value, never need polishing, and could never be stolen from me. And I almost missed it entirely.

I found my true treasure when I finally decided to let go of what I thought was my treasure so I could cling to the promise that God alone was enough for me.

True Treasure

Jesus told a simple parable to teach his followers the meaning of true treasure: "The kingdom of heaven is like treasure hidden in a field. When a man found it, he hid it again, and then in his joy went and sold all he had and bought that field" (Matthew 13:44).

When you find true treasure, you're willing to sacrifice for it, even if it seems counterintuitive. And what this man did definitely seemed counterintuitive at first glance. I mean, when your goal is to have much, does it really make sense to let go of everything you've worked so hard to gain? The man's family and friends probably thought he was nuts. But to him, the sacrifice made complete sense. In fact, it likely didn't even seem like a sacrifice; he was simply trading up—way up!

When the man sold everything he had and let go of what he previously thought was his treasure, he freed himself up to gain so much more. It wasn't a sacrifice because he now viewed everything he'd once had as mere trinkets in comparison to true treasure. That's what happens when we allow ourselves to see Jesus for everything he is—it becomes clear how comparatively dull our earthly treasure is. It's really only a faint glimmer of what we receive when we make Christ alone our greatest treasure. And it's only after realizing the richness of Christ—the everlasting value of his forgiveness, goodness, love, and holiness—that we can truly start to let go of the treasures we once fought for and held on to so tightly. When we realize the richness of Christ, he is what we grasp tightly and say, "If I have Christ, then I have everything." These are the riches the apostle Paul referred to when he wrote, "My God will meet all your needs according to the riches of his glory in Christ Jesus" (Philippians 4:19).

That's not to say that there's anything inherently wrong with earthly treasures. Quite the opposite. God designed marriage and family, and he wants us to find joy in them. But when these or any other earthly treasures displace God as our source of security and identity, they become idols. We know we've created an idol when we value the gift more than the God who created and gave us the gift. And that can happen even in marriage when we look to a spouse rather than to God as our true treasure.

In the parable, it's important to note that Jesus says the man "*in his joy* went and sold all he had" (emphasis added). It's like when Josh and I tell our kids they can have a bowl of ice cream for dessert if they clean up their toys. Any other time we ask them to clean up, we might hear the typical moaning and groaning. But if ice cream is part of the deal? It's, "Sure thing, Mom and Dad! No problem!" Cleaning up toys is suddenly an opportunity rather than a chore. They actually get excited because they know their work will be worth it—ice cream will be waiting for them when it's all said and done.

I think that's something like what Jesus is describing. Work was required of the man—he had to let go of all he had—but he knew it would be worth it. *So* worth it. And that's the promise Jesus makes to us—that we can have joy even as we do the hard work of letting go of lesser treasures, because he is worth it.

What's interesting to me is the brief period when the man

had nothing. Between the time he sold everything and bought the field, he had absolutely nothing to fall back on. During that in-between time, he put his faith entirely in the treasure he was *going* to have. And that was more than enough to sustain his joy.

We need to remember this when we enter our own in-between period of exchanging earthly treasures for true treasure. We may be in a period of waiting, but we also know that the treasure in the field—the promise of eternal life with Christ—is ours. Even though we're not able to experience the fullness of that treasure while we remain on earth, we can still choose to live in fullness of joy.

You might be wondering, *But how can I know if something is actually an idol in my life and I'm not just enjoying a good gift?* Here's a question to get you started: How would you respond and feel if that good gift were taken away? For example, let's say your treasure is security. Well, that could take many forms. For the younger version of myself, security looked like finding a husband. For others, security might be a well-paying job, praise and acceptance, or a retirement nest egg. Whatever it is for you, how would you feel if, tomorrow, for whatever reason, you no longer had it?

Of course, losing any earthly treasure would be extremely painful and difficult to navigate. Jesus never asks us to be apathetic about our relationships or supporting ourselves and our families. But no job or retirement plan can save us, and no human being can stick around forever. And if losing any of these things would cause you to lose yourself—to feel you had no identity or purpose without them—then you may be clinging to an idol for a false sense of security rather than as enjoyment of a good gift. That's what I did when I relied on my one person—my brother, a best friend, a boyfriend, and even my husband—to be my treasure.

If, like me, you've hoped that your marriage and your spouse would be your ultimate and consistent source of happiness and fulfillment, and you're now thinking, *I knew marriage would be hard at times, but I didn't think it would be* this *hard*, then I have good news for you. You don't have to start over with someone new to find what you're looking for. And fixing your spouse, even if that were possible, isn't the answer. The starting point is a treasure hunt, one that takes place in your own heart.

Savannah's Story of Surrendering an Idol

"My husband and I were just nineteen when we got married and started having kids. We were so young and had no idea what we were doing. I had a miscarriage and then gave birth to our first baby before our first anniversary. We lived in a tiny trailer, I was still in college, and my husband worked long hard hours as a logger. It was all overwhelming. We weren't carefree like we had been when we were dating, and I felt so much distance between us. We fought about money and didn't see eye to eye when it came to discipline for our child. My husband withdrew emotionally, and I withdrew physically. Our resentment toward each other grew, and I eventually discovered he was using social media to talk to other girls.

"I left to stay with my parents, met with a lawyer, and started the divorce process. It was almost five years into our marriage, and I was also pregnant with our second child.

Even after everything we had been through, I still loved my husband and didn't want to let him go. I was in so much pain, and yet this was the situation that completely changed my relationship with God. Although I had grown up as a Christian, my relationship with God up until that point had been at a very superficial level. I cried out to him so much during this time, and it was the first time I ever realized I could hear him speak back to me.

"At first, I sensed him saying that I had made my husband an idol. I needed to give him up and let God be enough for me. I finally made it to the point where I felt ready to let my husband go and just rely on God. It was a hard but beautiful choice. Once my husband was no longer an idol, I sensed God telling me that I could stay with him after all. I felt like Abraham must have felt when he was preparing to sacrifice his son Isaac but then was stopped at the last minute.

"When my husband and I decided to start working on our marriage, our arguments changed from screaming, throwing things, and saying hurtful words to calm discussions. I no longer withheld intimacy as a weapon or punishment, and my husband and I grew closer emotionally. My relationship with God has grown so much since then, and he has also shown me how to be a better wife. It's amazing what God can do when we surrender our idols to him."

Treasures in Heaven

Jesus often taught how fleeting earthly treasures are when compared to the treasures that await us in heaven:

> Do not store up for yourselves treasures on earth, where moths and vermin destroy, and where thieves break in and steal. But store up for yourselves treasures in heaven, where moths and vermin do not destroy, and where thieves do not break in and steal. For where your treasure is, there your heart will be also. (Matthew 6:19–21)

We need to love and cherish our spouses, but we must guard against making them our ultimate treasure. Loving our spouses and wanting security and happiness are not sinful desires. But without Christ guiding us to place them in the proper perspective, we risk putting our spouses on a pedestal and granting them undue influence over our lives. That's because our treasure— whatever or whomever it may be—can become our primary source of identity, significance, and security. It can be what drives us and motivates us. And to put all that on another human being is too much. Like a plant that wilts when it's overwatered, we can overwhelm the things and people we hold dear if we make them our ultimate treasure and cling to them too tightly. Instead, Christ says to go ahead and get married and love your spouse. But let Christ be the foundation for loving them well by loving him above all.

I love how C. S. Lewis puts it in a quote we framed and hung in the stairwell of our home:

> When I have learnt to love God better than my earthly dearest, I shall love my earthly dearest better than I do now. In so far as I learn to love my earthly dearest at the expense of God and *instead* of God, I shall be moving towards the state in which I shall not love my earthly dearest at all. When

first things are put first, second things are not suppressed but increased.[1]

No human being, not even a spouse, is meant to fully satisfy the deepest longings of our hearts. So go on a treasure hunt and take a closer look at what matters most to you. Consider what truly shapes your day-to-day decisions—how you invest your time and resources, how you view and treat your spouse, and even the thoughts that occupy your mind throughout the day. Underneath it all is your earthly dearest, the treasure that holds sway over your heart. And God invites you to surrender whatever that is so you can love him more.

Reflection

- When you were growing up, what did you rely on most for a sense of security and identity? For example, was it a person, a place, something you enjoyed or were good at? In what ways, if any, have you continued to rely on whatever that was for a sense of security and identity as an adult?

- True treasure is something we're willing to sacrifice for, even when it seems counterintuitive. What might the sacrifices you've made, recently or in the past, reveal about what your true treasure is?

---

1. Walter Hooper, ed., *The Collected Letters of C. S. Lewis: Narnia, Cambridge, and Joy 1950–1963*, vol. 3 (New York: HarperCollins, 2007), 247, italics in original.

- In what ways does Jesus' parable of the treasure in the field challenge you? In what ways does it encourage you?

- Look ahead to the time you and your spouse will spend together in the next twenty-four hours. In those moments, what might it look like in practical terms to love your spouse better by loving God better, as C. S. Lewis described?

Prayer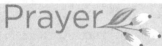

Ask God to:

- search your heart and help you identify the unfulfilled desires that have become unmet expectations or sources of resentment in your marriage. Surrender those desires to him as an acknowledgment that you want him alone to be your greatest treasure.

- forgive you for allowing your spouse, or any expectations you had of them, to displace God as your true treasure.

- reveal his richness to you so he can truly be the greatest treasure in your life.

CHAPTER 2

The Root of Selfishness

was wiping down counters after volunteering to serve breakfast at church one Sunday morning when I struck up a
conversation with a grad student a few years older than me
who was also volunteering. He'd heard I had a blog and asked
what I wrote about.

"Mostly marriage and family," I said, not going into too much
detail. I figured the topics wouldn't be that interesting to him
since he was single.

"That's awesome!" he said, his eyes brightening. "I'm actually
studying counseling. I want to be a marriage counselor."

"Oh, wow!" I said, surprised and curious since he wasn't
married.

"You know, I have this theory about marriage problems,"
he said.

"Oh yeah?" I said, raising my eyebrows and waiting to hear
what he eagerly wanted to share.

"I believe every problem in marriage boils down to one
issue," he said, pausing for dramatic effect. "Communication."

"You really think so?" I asked.

"Totally!" he said. "Think about it. Issues with finances, feeling underappreciated, disagreeing on important issues—they can all be solved with communication."

I did think about it. And I continued to think about it while I finished cleaning up. His theory didn't sit right with me, but I couldn't put my finger on why. *No way do half of the marriages in the US end just because of communication issues*, I thought. Josh and I had been married for a few years at that point, and we were pretty good at talking things out. Even so, our marriage wasn't always easy.

At home that afternoon, I talked it through with Josh. "He's wrong," I said, wishing I had come up with an intelligent response a lot sooner (story of my life) so I could have told him just *how* wrong he was. "It sounds really nice," I said, "but, unfortunately, it's just not that simple. And if he ever gets married, he'll learn that sooner or later. Everyone does."

Josh listened while I ranted.

"What about different family upbringings?" I huffed. "Or addictions, past hurts, or different values? Sure, communication would help a lot with those things. But talking it out isn't going to solve *everything*. Marriage is so much more complicated than that." After going on for a few more minutes, I realized I did agree with the grad student from church on one thing—most relational problems were rooted in a single issue, but it wasn't communication. When I looked at other sources of marital difficulty, I could trace almost all of them back to one thing—selfishness. And selfishness plays an immense role in making marriage complicated, messy, and hard.

The Root of the Problem

A friend, I'll call her Ahna, once told me how frustrated she was that her husband, Brian, never took out the trash unless she asked. Whenever she did ask, he happily did so without complaining, but the fact that she had to *ask* irked her. What she wanted was for Brian to take responsibility for taking out the trash; instead, it felt to Ahna as if Brian thought he was doing her a favor. Brian did help around the house in other ways. When he was done working for the day, he often helped with dinner and with the baby and did the yard work. However, Ahna was raised in a home in which taking out the trash was the man's responsibility. Plus, a full bag of trash was heavy and awkward for her to carry, so she expected Brian to take on the weekly task without having to be asked.

When Ahna tried talking to Brian about this, his answer was unsatisfying. "I'm sorry," he said. "I know I forget to take it out a lot. I'll try to be better about remembering. But honestly, I'm probably going to need reminders from you. And then I'll be happy to do it." Ugh. This was precisely what Ahna did not want to have to do.

A few weeks later, Ahna decided to stop asking. Still frustrated by the way the reminders made her feel (after all, it's not like he had to remind her to do *her* chores, so why did she have to carry that mental load for *him*?), she wanted to see what would happen if she never reminded Brian. Each Sunday night, Ahna waited to see if Brian would remember on his own. Once she was sure he had forgotten, she would take out the trash herself without a word, all the while stewing: *I knew he'd forget again.*

After a few more weeks of this, Ahna grudgingly asked Brian to take out the trash again. Brian said, "Yeah, I'll take it out. Thanks for taking it out for me the last few weeks. Why haven't you been asking me to do it?"

"Because I wanted to see if you would remember to do it yourself," Ahna said in a steamy tone.

Brian paused for a second as his emotions turned from gratitude to defensiveness. "So these last few weeks, you've just been watching me and testing me?" It was a question, but he said it like a hurtful accusation.

Ahna pursed her lips, not wanting to admit the truth. Instead, she circled back to the origins of her resentment. "It just feels like you think you're doing me a favor when, obviously, we both use the trash and it's heavy for me to take out."

And on and on the argument went.

Eventually, Ahna apologized for testing Brian and holding his forgetfulness over his head in bitterness. She agreed again to remind him without taking it personally because she knew he loved her. Brian agreed again to do a better job of remembering on his own by setting a reminder on his phone. Ahna decided that taking out the trash wasn't a big enough issue to cause resentment between them, and they both decided to work together to choose selflessness, especially in those inevitable times when the other dropped the ball.

What's ironic is that my friends actually had decent communication. Ahna communicated her expectations and feelings, and Brian communicated his needs. So while good communication is important, it didn't solve their problem, which was rooted in selfishness.

Selfishness causes us to look out for our own interests and

overlook our spouse's and, well, anyone else's, which can cause a world of pain if everyone were to live that way all the time. Which, if we're honest, is often the case.

Selfishness causes us to prioritize ourselves. Nineteenth-century poet Oscar Wilde said it well: "Selfishness is not living as one wishes to live, it is asking others to live as one wishes to live."[1] Whether or not we realize it, our human nature works extremely hard to make sure we have the comfort, admiration, and respect we feel we need and deserve, and it doesn't mind overlooking the needs of others to get it.

Selfishness can be especially difficult to recognize in ourselves—and even more difficult to overcome—especially in Western cultures that have a hyperfixation on self, autonomy, and individuality. If I put others down and belittle them for the sake of standing up for myself, I simply "know my worth." If I leave relationships the moment they stop serving me, I'm only "setting boundaries." I've noticed a whiff of this even in worship songs with phrases such as, "Your [God's] thoughts are of me," "I am enough," or, "You didn't want heaven without us." Even as believers, we can easily fall into thinking that we are the most important thing; that we need to look out for our own best interests above all else; and that others, or even God, should be doing the same.

It was selfishness that was at the root of Ahna's frustration with Brian because she felt she deserved a partner who took responsibility for taking out the trash. And it was selfishness at the root of Brian's unwillingness to remember to take out the trash on his own because he essentially wanted it to remain

---

1. Oscar Wilde, "The Soul of Man," in *The Soul of Man and Prison Writings*, ed. Isobel Murray, Oxford World's Classics (Oxford: Oxford University Press, 1990), 32.

Ahna's responsibility. Both fell into a habit of doing what was best—or easiest—for themselves rather than for their spouse.

While communication is an essential tool for helping us unravel a tangled thread of issues and conflicts in our relationship, it's never going to be a magic wand that makes all selfish motives disappear. Selfishness is the feeling that says, *Nothing matters more than what I want and think I need,* and it often creates barriers to growth in our relationships.

Selfishness Assessment

Selfishness can be tricky to recognize in ourselves because we tend to feel like our motives are well-intentioned and therefore justified. What marks an action as selfish is not our intentions but our failure to consider or our intentional disregard of the impact our choices have on others.

Listed below are nine examples of characteristically selfish behaviors. Although there may be exceptions, if you catch yourself engaging in these behaviors, chances are high that selfishness is at work. As you read through the list, consider any recent behaviors or tendencies you recognize in yourself.

You may be acting selfishly if you:

- **Quickly move past your spouse's feelings.** Dismissing, downplaying, or ignoring your spouse's genuine emotions or concerns is almost always a selfish behavior, even if you feel you have a good reason for doing so. Failing to empathize or offer emotional support is hurtful.

- **Make a major decision unilaterally.** Making significant decisions, such as financial choices or life changes, without consulting your spouse or seeking their input is typically a sign of selfishness. This is true even if you think the decision will benefit you both.
- **Withhold affection or attention to get what you want.** Withholding or threatening to withhold affection, intimacy, or attention as a means of control or manipulation reflects selfish motives that can harm your marriage.
- **Consistently put your own needs first.** Prioritizing only your own needs, wants, and comfort in everyday situations without considering or caring how your choices affect your spouse is selfish behavior.
- **Refuse to compromise.** An unwillingness to compromise, even on minor issues, is an indication of selfishness. A healthy marriage requires give-and-take from both partners.
- **Fail to show appreciation.** Failing to express gratitude or appreciation for your spouse's efforts and contributions in your relationship can leave them feeling unvalued and unimportant.
- **Avoid taking responsibility.** Shifting blame, avoiding accountability, or refusing to take responsibility for your actions are selfish behaviors that erode trust and accountability in marriage.
- **React defensively.** Regularly reacting defensively to feedback or criticism from your spouse—rather than considering their perspective and working toward a resolution—is a mark of selfishness.

- **Diminish or fail to support your spouse's goals.** Consistently disregarding your spouse's goals, dreams, and aspirations demonstrates a self-centered posture to a relationship. Ideally, we should be our spouse's biggest cheerleader.

We all battle selfishness sometimes, and recognizing yourself in one or more these behaviors doesn't mean you are a "selfish person." However, when a behavior becomes habitual, it's worth taking a closer look at what's driving that behavior so you can surrender whatever it is to Christ, work toward building a more selfless attitude, and live in greater unity and understanding with your spouse.

Selfishness Creates Barriers

A barrier is an obstacle to progress. Within marriage, selfishness is a barrier that keeps us from moving toward the relationship we want. Although it causes a lot of pain, it can be difficult to recognize because it's sometimes disguised as other behaviors and choices. However, when we boil it down, we can see that selfishness in marriage often manifests as two specific barriers—overgrown self-importance and blame.

Overgrown Self-Importance

The first picture the Bible gives of overgrown or exaggerated self-importance takes place in a conversation between Eve and Satan, who appears in the form of a serpent.

The woman said to the serpent, "We may eat the fruit from the trees in the garden. But about the fruit of the tree in the middle of the garden, God said, 'You must not eat it or touch it, or you will die.'"

"No! You will not die," the serpent said to the woman. "In fact, God knows that when you eat it *your eyes will be opened and you will be like God*, knowing good and evil." Then the woman saw that the tree was good for food and delightful to look at, and that it was desirable for obtaining wisdom. So she took some of its fruit and ate it; she also gave some to her husband, who was with her, and he ate it. Then the eyes of both of them were opened, and they knew they were naked; so they sewed fig leaves together and made loincloths for themselves. (Genesis 3:2–7 HCSB, emphasis added)

When Eve heard she could become like God—autonomous and wise—she decided nothing mattered more than that, and her exaggerated sense of self-importance made the serpent's proposition too good to pass up. Adam's and Eve's eyes were indeed opened when they ate the fruit, but what they saw in themselves was their depravity, not their divinity.

We often have self-important views of ourselves too, thinking we're mostly good, have good intentions, or are generally better than others. But the Bible consistently challenges our self-delusions because as long as we think we're mostly good, we forget just how much we need God.

The prophet Isaiah wrote that even the good we try to do falls far short: "All of us have become like one who is unclean, and all our righteous acts are like filthy rags" (Isaiah 64:6). Why does he say that even our own righteousness is filthy? It feels a little defeating, right? But if we look deep down to the motives behind those good deeds, they can often be traced back to selfish intentions.

If I work hard at my job, I'll gain recognition.

If I surprise my spouse by cleaning up the whole house, they'll show me more affection.

If I serve in my church, I'll look and feel like a good Christian.

Even seemingly selfless things can be done with selfish motives. And we sometimes approach our relationship with God in the same way. When the job is more frustrating than it is rewarding, when the kids are struggling in school, when the marriage isn't as joyful as it once was, we often ask God why *we* have to deal with these things—as if we, for some reason, don't deserve hardships or struggles.

The Bible challenges our ideas of exaggerated self-importance, reminding us that even our own righteousness can be traced back to selfish intentions. Scripture encourages us to see ourselves—and our motives—with eyes wide open, and to examine our hearts before God: "A person may think their own ways are right, but the LORD weighs the heart" (Proverbs 21:2).

Blame

Because selfishness causes us to place disproportionate value and priority on ourselves, when things don't turn out like we hoped or the consequences of our selfishness make life difficult, we're often quick to blame the people around us. "If only my husband were more (fill in the blank)." "If only my wife were less _____." That was certainly the case in the Garden of Eden when God asked Adam and Eve if they had eaten the forbidden fruit—Adam blamed Eve, and Eve blamed the serpent (Genesis 3:11–13).

But the Bible also offers another compelling story of blame as a barrier. This one takes place in the life of Job, and what makes it different from the Adam and Eve story is that the person Job blames for his hardships is God himself.

Job was a wealthy landowner whom the Bible describes as "the greatest man among all the people of the East" (Job 1:3). In addition to Job's great wealth, the Bible also describes him as having a sterling character: "This man was blameless and upright; he feared God and shunned evil" (1:1). And yet when Job experiences profound loss and suffering, it is this very view of himself as blameless that becomes a barrier in his relationship to God.

When Job presents his case to God, detailing all the ways his tremendously difficult circumstances are unjustified, he makes a point of reminding God that he is blameless. And it's clear from his argument that not only is Job angry about his suffering, but he also believes his righteousness should afford him an easier life—one without struggle or loss.

> "If I have walked with falsehood
>   or my foot has hurried after deceit—
> let God weigh me in honest scales
>   and he will know that I am blameless. . . .
> If I have denied the desires of the poor
>   or let the eyes of the widow grow weary,
> if I have kept my bread to myself,
>   not sharing it with the fatherless—
> but from my youth I reared them as a father
>   would,

and from my birth I guided the widow."
(Job 31:5–6, 16–18)

Job is essentially saying, "What possible reason could there be for such suffering when I am good and blameless in every way?" Even Job's close friends eventually stop trying to give him advice, seeing that it's useless because Job sees himself as above reproach: "So these three men stopped answering Job, because he was righteous in his own eyes" (Job 32:1). And yet if there's one thing Job's story shows us, it's that our righteousness is nothing compared to God's holiness. God's holiness requires that we confront our own brokenness and admit that *we* are the problem. It isn't until Job encounters God's holiness that he finally sees himself for what and who he truly is—unworthy.

The LORD said to Job:

"Will the one who contends with the Almighty
    correct him?
Let him who accuses God answer him!"

Then Job answered the LORD:

"I am unworthy—how can I reply to you?
    I put my hand over my mouth.
I spoke once, but I have no answer—
    twice, but I will say no more." (Job 40:1–5)

God takes his time showing Job just how big he, God, is—and how his plans won't always be compatible with Job's (Job

38–41). In other words, God doesn't fit in Job's box. And God won't conform to Job's human expectations of how he thinks he should be rewarded for his good character or his good deeds. When Job finally understands his righteousness in comparison to God's holiness, he says to God:

> "I know that you can do all things;
>> no purpose of yours can be thwarted.
>
> You asked, 'Who is this that obscures my plans
>> without knowledge?'
>> Surely I spoke of things I did not understand,
>> Things too wonderful for me to know.
>
> You said, 'Listen now, and I will speak;
>> I will question you,
>> and you shall answer me.'
>
> My ears had heard of you
>> but now my eyes have seen you.
>
> Therefore I despise myself
>> and repent in dust and ashes." (Job 42:2–6)

We know we're on our way to understanding our true condition before God when we recognize our sinfulness and acknowledge that we're lost. That's when we realize what we're truly capable of—and not in a good way—and decide to cling to God and *his* goodness instead of our own. After his encounter with God, Job was profoundly humbled. He went from bragging about his blamelessness to saying he despised himself!

Like Job, when we are faced with adversity, our mistakes, or the consequences of our own selfishness, our ego strives to protect itself by deflecting responsibility for our circumstances onto others. We find it challenging to face up to our own flaws, weaknesses, or wrongdoings, fearing that such an acknowledgment may tarnish the facade of perfection we seek to uphold.

Asserting our own blamelessness by blaming others, our circumstances, or God can be viewed as a defense mechanism—a way to preserve our self-image and escape the discomfort of owning up to our true condition. By shifting blame away from us, we protect ourselves with a false sense of superiority, convincing ourselves that we are both faultless and worthy of better treatment.

Both exaggerated self-importance and blame are barriers that hinder personal growth and stunt relationships. The way forward lies in understanding our true condition before God, practicing humility, and being willing to learn from our mistakes. That's how we begin to embrace the selflessness that every marriage needs in order to thrive.

Hearts Set on Christ

When we begin to grasp God's holiness, we no longer serve God, others, or our spouse to earn things for ourselves. Instead, we choose to serve God because we want to know him, delight in him, and be close to him. Instead of using God to get what we think we deserve based on our own merits, we want God to use us for his own purposes.

This same dynamic translates beautifully into a godly marriage. If both you and your spouse are unwilling to acknowledge your own selfishness and brokenness, all the communication in the world isn't going to solve your problems. But if you have a humble view of yourself, desire to meet the needs of your spouse, and seek out God's goodness for both of you, it leads to loving, sacrificial service. That way, instead of asking, *Why can't my spouse be more* _____ *for me?*, you naturally ask, *How can we best glorify God together?*

As you embark on this journey of understanding God's holiness and embracing selflessness, may you discover the transformative power it holds for you, both individually and as a couple. With God at the center of your marriage, your hearts and your relationship are poised to flourish, and you can embrace the joyous purpose of glorifying God together in every aspect of your journey.

Reflection

- Ahna and Brian had a conflict they thought was about taking out the trash, but underneath it all was a root of selfishness. When you consider recent conflicts with your spouse, how would you describe the root of selfishness underneath it all? In what ways did both of you prioritize your own interests first?

- Exaggerated self-importance leads us to believe we are mostly good, have good intentions, and are generally better than others. In what ways, if any, do you recognize this mindset in yourself? How has it led to conflict in your marriage?

- We often use blame to deflect responsibility for our circumstances onto others. When recently have you blamed God or others for what you were going through? How were you trying to protect yourself or avoid facing up to your own flaws, weaknesses, or wrongdoing?

- Embracing selflessness includes understanding our true condition before God, practicing humility, and being willing to learn from our mistakes. What comes to mind when you think about applying these three things to your marriage?

Prayer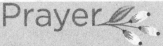

Ask God to:

- help you cultivate a realistic and humble view of yourself.

- help you practice sacrificial service in your marriage and prioritize glorifying him in your relationship.

- reveal any selfishness in your heart and help you prioritize his will as well as the needs of your spouse over your own desires.

- enable you to see your spouse as God sees them and to love them with the same kind of sacrificial love that Christ has shown you.

CHAPTER 3

I Would Never

I was almost finished with the last touches on my new home office. Our one-year-old daughter, Evy, was crawling around the foot of my desk and three-year-old David was jumping from cushion to cushion on the couch nearby. I looked at them and felt a small ache in my chest starting to well up but then quickly moved on and finished setting up.

The next day, I was starting my first "real job," one I could do from home, and I wanted to be as prepared as I could be. Everything had to be perfect and running smoothly. The idea of messing up or sounding silly to my new boss and colleagues terrified me. So the more prepared I felt, the more confident I felt too.

Truth be told, even though I could still wear my sweatpants to Monday morning meetings and help get lunch for the kids in the afternoons, I was reluctant to enter the corporate world, and I hoped the job would be temporary. When Josh lost his job a couple months earlier and had difficulty finding a new one, I decided to pick up some work to help support our family in the meantime.

Fast-forward to a year later, and not only was I still working my corporate job, but I was also really good at it! Josh and I had officially swapped roles of stay-at-home-parent and breadwinner. But the small ache in my chest I had felt when I looked at Evy and David never went away. In fact, it grew.

I kept Josh up late at night, brainstorming through tears, trying to manipulate scenarios in which I could work less and be with the kids more. But in every scenario, we came full circle. With my newfound career, it was just a fact that I had much more earning potential than Josh. We were also working toward saving for our first home, and I couldn't just throw that dream away.

Being a stay-at-home mom was all I had ever wanted to be. And while I was extremely proud of myself and my accomplishments, I longed for what I couldn't have. So I remained working and Josh remained the kids' primary caregiver.

More months went by, and the ache of sadness in my chest turned into bitterness. I looked at Josh with resentment. *How could he? How could he just take my dream? I would never do that to him. I would have found a way.*

Most of the time my anger burned like a dim ember, but it could easily flare up at the slightest disagreement, inconvenience, or reminder that what I wanted was never going to be my reality. While it was invisible to me at the time, my pride grew right alongside my resentment—which led me to think of myself as the better person in our relationship—and it clouded my perception of both Josh and myself.

Clouded Self-Perception

Author Stephen Covey has a powerful quote about clouded self-perception: "We judge ourselves by our intentions and others by their behavior."[1] The first time I read this, I thought, *Oh my goodness, yes! That is so true!* And while I wanted to believe that I, of course, was the exception to the rule, I knew I did this too.

I mean, when we're wronged, what's the first thing we do? If someone wrongs me, I go straight to Josh, slap my hand on the counter, and say, "You would not *believe* what just happened to me!" Or if Josh is the one who committed the wrong, I tend to mope around in victimhood while dropping subtle hints that we are "not okay" and he needs to make up for whatever he did. And I'm probably not alone in this.

We love to feel like we would never stoop down to the level of [*fill in the blank with whatever behavior we feel is beneath us*]. And everyone does this. Members of opposing political parties look at each other and think, *I would never vote that way.* Kids look at their parents and think, *I would never put my kids in time-out.* Parents look at other parents and think, *I would never let my children behave that way.* And husbands and wives look at each other and think, *I would never treat someone that way,* or *I would have done that better.* But all along, we fail to put ourselves in the other person's shoes, understand the greater context surrounding their choices, pick up on the nuances surrounding their situation, or consider how their background may have influenced their decision or behavior.

Where does the "I would never" impulse come from? It's simple—pride. Pride whispers in our ears and tells us we're not as bad as others, and *especially* not as bad as the people who need our forgiveness.

---

1. Stephen Covey, *The Speed of Trust: The One Thing That Changes Everything* (New York: Simon & Schuster, 2018), 13.

This kind of pride can be especially challenging for those of us who grew up in church. I remember the time my high school youth pastor asked me to share my testimony at an upcoming youth group meeting. I had heard testimonies of God's grace in the lives of Christians who'd overcome things like addictions, jail sentences, and secret sins. I was always amazed at how the grace of God was working in their lives in such obvious and powerful ways. Everyone could see how grace had changed them, plain as day.

But me? I grew up in a Christian family and was afraid to even think about coming home after curfew. Of course, I knew God had saved me from my sin, but I didn't have a dramatic testimony to prove it. I hadn't been as bad as they were, so it seemed like my life hadn't really changed all that much. I told my youth pastor I didn't feel worthy to share my testimony.

What I didn't realize at the time was that while I was saying I didn't feel worthy of sharing the story of how Christ had worked in my life, my pride was keeping me from fully realizing just how much I had *needed* saving—that there was no difference between my spiritual condition and the spiritual condition of those who had more dramatic testimonies.

Years later, when I struggled with not being the stay-at-home parent, it was this same pride that convinced me *I* would never have done such a thing to Josh. And it's the same pride that makes all of us think, *Okay, yeah, I know I need forgiveness, but* those *people—my neighbor, my parents, my spouse—they really need it.*

The good news is that long before we could ever recognize pride in ourselves, God knew it was there. He knew how dire our situation was, that we had no ability to save ourselves, and that we had no idea just how much we needed to be saved. The apostle Paul wrote about this some two thousand years ago in his letter to believers at the church in Ephesus:

> And you were dead in your trespasses and sins in which you previously walked according to the ways of this world, according to the ruler who exercises authority over the lower heavens, the spirit now working in the disobedient. We too all previously lived among them in our fleshly desires, carrying out the inclinations of our flesh and thoughts, and we were by nature children under wrath as the others were also. But God, who is rich in mercy, because of His great love that He had for us, made us alive with the Messiah even though we were dead in trespasses. You are saved by grace! Together with Christ Jesus He also raised us up and seated us in the heavens, so that in the coming ages He might display the immeasurable riches of His grace through His kindness to us in Christ Jesus. For you are saved by grace through faith, and this is not from yourselves; it is God's gift—not from works, *so that no one can boast.* For we are His creation, created in Christ Jesus for good works, which God prepared ahead of time so that we should walk in them. (Ephesians 2:1–10 HCSB, emphasis added)

Paul starts out by saying we were spiritually *dead.* People who are dead can't call for help; they can't work harder to gain God's approval; and they certainly can't save themselves. They are completely and utterly helpless. But God, in his mercy, raised us—you and me (not just those with addictions, jail sentences, and secret sins)—from the dead when Jesus rose from the dead and gave us a seat in the heavens. Notice how all the verbs are in the past tense. In other words, this work of God is already done. There is literally nothing left *to* do. Your place—and every other believer's place—next to the Father is already secured.

Why did God do it this way? Why did he make it so we don't need to earn our seat next to him in heaven? *So that no one can boast.* He did it precisely so that none of us could take *any* credit for our salvation and relationship with God. Whether you were a Christian from a young age and have lived most of your life trying to honor God or whether you've spent most of your life in outright sin and rebellion, you were once completely dead and helpless in sin. You have been made alive through Christ alone.

If it makes you feel any better, we're not the first generation of people who have forgotten their desperate need for God's grace in their lives. Take a look at how Jesus responded to several self-righteous religious leaders when they confronted him with a woman who was clearly living in sin:

> At dawn he appeared again in the temple courts, where all the people gathered around him, and he sat down to teach them. The teachers of the law and the Pharisees brought in a woman caught in adultery. They made her stand before the group and said to Jesus, "Teacher, this woman was caught in the act of adultery. In the Law Moses commanded us to stone such women. Now what do you say?" They were using this question as a trap, in order to have a basis for accusing him.
>
> But Jesus bent down and started to write on the ground with his finger. When they kept on questioning him, he straightened up and said to them, "Let any one of you who

is without sin be the first to throw a stone at her." Again he stooped down and wrote on the ground.

At this, those who heard began to go away one at a time, the older ones first, until only Jesus was left, with the woman still standing there. Jesus straightened up and asked her, "Woman, where are they? Has no one condemned you?"

"No one, sir," she said.

"Then neither do I condemn you," Jesus declared. "Go now and leave your life of sin." (John 8:2–11)

I find it interesting that it was the oldest religious leaders who were the first to admit they hadn't lived a life without sin. They evidently had a much more realistic view of themselves and their imperfections. And yet it was these same Pharisees—leaders who had dedicated their lives to earning salvation through adherence to the Law—who were the first to accuse this woman of sin. Their pride clouded both their self-perception and their view of others to the point that they couldn't even fathom how they needed grace just as much as this woman did. Jesus had to remind them that, while our sins may look different, we are all born separated from God and in need of God's grace.

Jesus Spent Time with Those Who Knew They Needed Him

There are so many stories throughout the Gospels in which Jesus intentionally spends time with those who were considered to be sinners—tax collectors, prostitutes, and other outcasts. No doubt there were times when even his disciples thought, *What on earth is he thinking by choosing to hang out with these people?*

What if someone sees us? And we might ask a similar question. Why *did* Jesus prioritize ministering to the outcasts and those blatantly living in sin? Wouldn't it have been easier to reach people who were already striving to be righteous?

As it turns out, the answer is no. In fact, Jesus shows us that the opposite is true. It's not the righteous but those who know how far from righteous they are who are most receptive to the gospel. And it is humility, not pride, that Jesus equates with greatness in the kingdom:

> At that time the disciples came to Jesus and asked, "Who is greatest in the kingdom of heaven?" Then He called a child to Him and had him standing among them. "I assure you," He said, "unless you are converted and become like children, you will never enter the kingdom of heaven. Therefore, whoever humbles himself like this child—this one is the greatest in the kingdom of heaven. And whoever welcomes one child like this in My name welcomes Me." (Matthew 18:1–5 HCSB)

Okay, from the outside it may not seem like little children and the outcasts Jesus ministered to have much in common, but Jesus begs to differ. He knows that both groups know just how needy they are. Children and outcasts know they need help. They are in a humble place and wear no rose-colored glasses that convince them they're good enough on their own—that they can save themselves and take care of themselves.

It's the outcasts and sinners who readily grasp the concept that they are dead in their sin and separated from God. And when they are healed by Jesus—physically, spiritually, or both—they are so amazed at God's grace that they celebrate it and glorify God because of it. Their joy and gratitude are great because they fully understand the magnitude of their need for God's grace.

Here's another way to think of it. Let's say you're going out of town, and you ask a friend to house-sit and feed your cat while you're away. When you come home, your friend sends you a text and says, "Hey, I didn't mean to snoop, but while I was house-sitting, I saw this bill on your kitchen counter, and, well, I decided to pay it for you."

How would you react in this situation? My guess is that it depends entirely on the size of the bill. If it was just a monthly internet bill, you might say, "Oh, wow, thank you! That's very kind of you." But if your friend paid off your student loans, mortgage, or five-figure credit card debt, you'd probably say something along the lines of, "Are you kidding me?! That's insane. Why would you even do that for me? Please tell me what I can do for you in return!" In both cases, your joy and gratitude are proportionate to the size of the gift.

The more we understand how much grace we've truly received, the more we rejoice in the fact that God gave us that grace as a gift we never could have earned. But if pride convinces us that we're better than others, that we just need a little forgiveness when we slip up here and there, we won't experience the full impact of God's grace in our lives. Pride distorts both our view of ourselves and our view of those who may have wronged us, making it appear as though we are on a pedestal and those other people are the ones who really need God's grace.

It wasn't until I was reminded of just how much I needed saving that I was able to see myself, and Josh, clearly. And the change didn't come until I asked Jesus for it. I asked that he humble me, remind me of how much I had been forgiven of, and help me to be gracious and loving to Josh. That's when I realized two things: (1) Josh hadn't actually done anything to wrong me; I just wasn't content in that season of life; and (2) all the while I was thinking, *I would never*, I was fooling myself into believing that I needed less grace than he did, even if I wouldn't have said so out loud. Again, "We judge ourselves by our intentions and others by their behavior."

I've seen this same type of clouded self-perception come over many other couples as well. I can't even tell you how many husbands and wives have written to me via my blog to share one thousand words on how terrible their spouse is. It often goes something like this: "I was rude to her that day, but it was only because I'd had a long day at work and now she hasn't talked to me in twenty-four hours and she's totally blowing it out of proportion and being so dramatic!"

The thing is, both husband and wife are prideful when they believe the other to be fundamentally worse than themselves. And as long as they're locked in that perception, they're nowhere close to admitting that they, too, need forgiveness from their spouse. Of course, there will be times when our spouses sin against or wrong us and we may have done nothing wrong at all. But what the Bible makes clear is that as much as Christ calls our spouses to repent and seek forgiveness, we, too, are called to be humble and forgive, remembering that we have already been forgiven much.

I got a reminder of just how important it is to have this kind of humility in marriage when Josh and I were on a missions trip several years back. At one point during our trip, we were chatting with our friends, one of whom was our pastor. When the conversation turned to the topic of my marriage blog, one of our friends asked me how I kept up with trying to give helpful suggestions for all the complicated problems people write in about. I said, "Honestly, it's not as complicated as you might think. I mean, there are a lot of messy problems, but they all boil down to one solution—believing that God and his grace are the only things you need." To that, our pastor-friend said a loud, "Amen!"

I was initially taken aback because I didn't think I had said anything groundbreaking. But when I reflected on it later, I thought, *Yeah, that* is *a big deal. Being not just content in Christ but rejoicing in Christ because of the fact that you were brought from death to life really changes your entire outlook on life, not to mention marriage—especially when it comes time for you to forgive others.*

That's why tax collectors and prostitutes were so receptive to Jesus—it was easy for them to see just how separated they were from God and how much they needed grace. When we see how far away we are from God, how unworthy we are of forgiveness, and how much we've been forgiven, it makes forgiving others that much simpler and easier.

Pulling Up Pride by the Roots

Our pride is what has us saying, *I'm not like them. I would never.* But grace is what tells us, "Actually, you are like them, and you would. But I have you covered." And the amazing thing we all tend to forget is that Christ, who is the only one who could have boasted in his righteousness, set the ultimate example for us:

Make your own attitude that of Christ Jesus,

> who, existing in the form of God,
> did not consider equality with God
> as something to be used for His own advantage.
> Instead He emptied Himself
> by assuming the form of a slave,
> taking on the likeness of men.
> And when He had come as a man,
> *He humbled Himself* by becoming obedient
> to the point of death—
> even to death on a cross. (Philippians 2:5–8
> HCSB, emphasis added)

It's because of Jesus' sacrifice that we can be made alive and have a place saved for us in heaven with Jesus next to the Father. Christ chose grace for us, for our spouses, and for anyone else who will accept it. And great freedom and confidence come from embracing that grace. Pastor and author Timothy Keller commented on this in his book *The Reason for God*:

> The Christian gospel is that I am so flawed that Jesus had to die for me, yet I am so loved and valued that Jesus was glad to die for me. This leads to deep humility and deep confidence at the same time. . . . I cannot feel superior to anyone, and yet I have nothing to prove to anyone. I do not think more of myself nor less of myself. Instead, I think of myself less.[2]

---

2. Timothy Keller, *The Reason for God: Belief in an Age of Skepticism* (New York: Dutton, 2008), 181.

Knowing that we are recipients of unmerited grace can be a source of great joy—joy when we are suffering or wronged and joy when things are going great. Grace enables us to have a humble view of ourselves, not looking down on others to feel better about ourselves but instead looking to Christ and being in awe of the greatness and mercy of God.

Reflection

- Can you recall recent situations in which you've thought to yourself, *I would never*? What insights might these situations reveal about how you view your spiritual condition and your need for grace?

- What comes to mind when you consider Stephen Covey's statement, "We judge ourselves by our intentions and others by their behavior"? In what ways, if any, do you recognize this dynamic in your marriage?

- How would you characterize your awareness of your need for grace in this season of your life? For example, is your awareness the highest it's ever been, the lowest, or somewhere in between? Why?

- What comes to mind when you think about showing more grace to your spouse? What makes that hard or easy for you to do?

- In what ways do you wish your spouse would show you more grace?

Prayer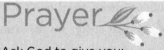

Ask God to give you:

- a deeper understanding of God's grace and love and the ability to extend that same grace and love to your spouse and others in your life.

- the strength to forgive others, just as Christ has forgiven you, so you can grow in your relationships, especially with your spouse.

- the strength to resist pride and to recognize and acknowledge your own shortcomings, so you can grow in your relationships with God and your spouse.

CHAPTER 4

When Anger Crops Up

s it possible to fold laundry in a threatening way? If so, I'm pretty sure I've done it. In fact, I may even have developed it into a carefully crafted skill, one I thought I was putting to good use not long ago.

It was Sunday afternoon, and the Seattle Seahawks had just made another first down. I was standing directly between the television and my husband, who was settled in on the couch, as I aggressively folded the shirt he had worn the day before.

My thoughts festered while trying to get Josh to make eye contact. *I wonder if he knows how his clothes end up back in his dresser. It's like he doesn't even notice all the things I do for him.* I was convinced that if we did make eye contact, he'd wake up out of his oblivious stupor of relaxation and Sunday football, apologize for not helping me sooner, and jump up to help. After all, weekends aren't just for relaxing; they're for getting everything done that's harder to get done during the week. Everybody knows that.

After more threatening folding and several failed attempts

to lock eyes, I resorted to increasingly louder huffs and puffs to break through the steady drone of the sports commentators.

"Um, are you okay?" Josh said, finally looking at me.

I inhaled and said, "I just wish I didn't have to ask you to help me." I exhaled, exasperated. I finally got my moment, except it didn't feel as satisfying as I thought it would.

His look said it all: *Okay, here we go again.*

And he was right.

Sure, he helped finish the laundry that day, but we were both angry, and no one was relaxing. The argument that followed ruined not only his enjoyment of the Seahawks game but the rest of our day as well.

Reaping What We Sow

We all have ideas in our heads of how certain things *should* go. If you consider yourself more of a type A person—someone who charges ahead and generally prefers more structure in your life—then you definitely have a few ideas of what your day should look like, who in your family is responsible for what, and how certain things (like loading the dishwasher) should happen. But even those of us who consider ourselves to be type B—who prefer a more go-with-the-flow approach to life—have lines that, when crossed, rub us the wrong way. If someone is being inflexible, hardheaded, or unsympathetic, it can really make us see red.

I've also found that the more we think an issue is black-and-white, the quicker we are to get angry about it, which makes sense. You wouldn't react the same way to your spouse forgetting to put the wet laundry in the dryer as you would to them coming home four hours late and not answering your texts in the meantime. That's because you can kind of understand forgetting the laundry—it's annoying, but you've been there too. But four hours late without so much as a text? That's a black-and-white case of wrongdoing. You can't even fathom doing such a thing, so you're instantly angry.

We all know the feeling of anger growing inside us. Sometimes it's a slow drip of observing annoying behaviors (like forgetting to put the laundry in the dryer) that eventually causes an outburst; other times it's a single spark that leads to an explosion.

When do you find yourself getting angry? When your spouse is inconsiderate? Inconsistent? Not valuing what's important to you? Whatever the cause may be, the gospel writer Luke helps us see the true origins of our anger. He lets us peer behind the veil to see what is truly causing our anger: "A good man brings good things out of the good stored up in his heart, and an evil man brings evil things out of the evil stored up in his heart. For the mouth speaks what the heart is full of" (Luke 6:45).

To be clear, the Bible doesn't equate all anger with sin. For example, James doesn't say we must never be angry, but instead that we should be "quick to hear, slow to speak, slow to anger" (James 1:19 HCSB). However, when anger is mentioned in the Bible, we're often asked to examine what the cause of our anger is. Jesus' statement in Luke 6 makes it clear that whatever comes out of our mouths, including anger, is an overflow of the heart. Or to put it another way, angry words and actions are our hearts spilling over. But what exactly *is* overflowing?

Let's say that one night, right before bedtime, the kids ask me and Josh if we can take them to the park in the morning. We look at each other, shrug, and say, "Yeah, that would work." Next thing we know, the kids are *bonkers*. They're wide-eyed, jumping around the bed, and it takes twenty to thirty minutes to get them to quiet down again and finally fall asleep.

The next morning, there's a downpour of rain. Not only that, but flashes of lightning burst across the sky every few minutes as well. We say to the kids, "We're really sorry, guys. We wanted to go to the park, but it's not safe to go during a lightning storm. We'll have to stay inside today."

They're devastated, angry, and resentful. You would think we had just told them they had thirty days to live. But that's how kids are—they don't yet have the perspective to see that not going to the park that particular morning actually isn't the end of the world. We could enjoy each other's company some other way—family movie night, making blanket forts, doing arts and crafts.

The thing is, while we as adults might not resort to throwing full-on temper tantrums, we can still have an extremely hard time coping when things don't go the way we hoped. And that is what overflows—the emotions we feel when we aren't able to secure what we truly desire. How do we respond when life doesn't work out in the ways we always dreamed it would? With fear, anger, sadness, or bitterness? Or with peace, content in the knowledge that, regardless of our current situation, God is good, and he will supply our needs?

Tending to Our Desires

We are driven by a multitude of desires, some of which may remain constant throughout our lifetime, while others change from one moment or season to the next. Beyond our basic needs for food, water, and shelter, we may desire respect from others, the comfort of rest after a long day, or the sense of security that comes from feeling taken care of. Some desires are physical, and others are emotional and psychological, such as the desire for love, admiration, or belonging.

Desires are an essential part of our lives, motivating us to pursue goals, happiness, and fulfillment. They are what fuel our drive for achievement and purpose. But when our desires are thwarted, we experience a wide range of emotions—from minor frustration or disappointment to anger or sadness.

Not only that, but we often try to hold on tighter to what we want when we think it might be taken from us. The story of Josh and me with the laundry is a simple, if not silly, example. I was angry because I felt like the chore of laundry shouldn't have to be solely my responsibility. In reality, though, it wasn't. At any other time, Josh would have been happy to help with the laundry. The pile of laundry started to bother me, and I decided to fold it at the exact moment Josh was relaxing. Plus, I was jealous that Josh was relaxing and I wasn't. Because I felt as though I was being made to choose between a clean home and resting on a Sunday afternoon, I held on to both desires even more tightly by being angry with Josh for not helping me get what I wanted when I wanted it. But there are often much weightier situations in which anger can overcome us when we start to see what we desire slipping away.

Our dear friends Jake and Kaitlyn struggled with infertility for years. God has since blessed them with two beautiful girls, but in their struggles to become pregnant, they told us they were forced to consider whether having a baby would truly cure what they felt was missing in their lives. In that extremely difficult time, they could have let their pain turn them away from each other or from God in anger. Instead, they were determined to cling to the hope they had in Christ, regardless of whether children would ever be part of their lives. They realized they had to bring their desires under submission to Christ and his will. When they eventually did have children, they felt even more blessed that God had given them such a wonderful gift—a gift they knew no one was ever promised or deserving of what they wanted.

It might come across as though I'm saying having desires is the core problem here. That's not the case, although Jesus did teach about self-denial and turning away from worldly desires. One of his most familiar teachings is this: "Whoever wants to be my disciple must deny themselves and take up their cross daily and follow me" (Luke 9:23). However, it's important to note that God doesn't expect us to *not* have desires. In fact, God himself desires to have a relationship with us. And because we're made in the image of God, we're naturally going to have desires too. That's a relief!

Although desires aren't sinful in and of themselves, when our earthly desires take precedence over our desire for God, they distract us from our calling of glorifying Christ. And sometimes even the best-intentioned desires can lead us astray if we pursue them in self-seeking ways. When our desires win the battle of our hearts, they become idols, and holding ourselves and others to Christ's standards becomes secondary.

The more time we spend with Christ, meditating on God's Word and drawing closer to him, the more our desires start to align with his desires. When our hearts are focused on glorifying Christ, our desires become less self-seeking and more focused on serving others. We start to value the things God values, such as love, grace, and compassion. And when we hold ourselves and others to Christ's standards, we are striving toward the ultimate goal of becoming more like him.

When I was angry that Josh didn't immediately forfeit his plans of watching the game to help me fold laundry, I was holding my husband to *my* standards (whatever I deemed them to be in that moment) to achieve what I desired—a clean home in which I could relax. Of course, there's nothing wrong with wanting a clean home, but the way I went about trying to achieve it led me into the sin of anger.

Take a look at what James says about this dynamic:

> What causes fights and quarrels among you? Don't they come from your desires that battle within you? . . .
>
> Submit yourselves, then, to God. Resist the devil, and he will flee from you. Come near to God and he will come near to you. Wash your hands, you sinners, and purify your hearts, you double-minded. (James 4:1, 7–8)

In addition to being blinded to our own selfish motives and pride, James states that we also have to contend with desires that are constantly *battling* within us. For example, the desire to be admired contends with the desire to make God great. The desire to rest vies with the desire to be present with our family. The desire to control outcomes fights with the desire to surrender outcomes to Christ. These and other battles wage war in our hearts every day, and if we don't surrender them to Christ—through prayer and asking for Christ's will to be done—they will inevitably lead us into anger and quarrels.

Declaring the Winner of Our Hearts

When I write something, I like Josh to read it so we can talk through what I'm working on; he's my first sounding board. After he read this chapter, he asked me to note in the laundry story that he should have been more attentive to my desires and wishes in that moment. Ideally, he would have laid down his desires to watch football and put me and our relationship before his desire to relax. And he's right. For any marriage to be truly happy, both parties are going to have to lay down their own desires from time to time.

However, the way to deal with conflicting desires in marriage isn't to simply forfeit your own desires so your spouse's desires can continuously trump yours. Instead, the invitation is for both you and your spouse to look at yourselves with eyes wide open. The goal is to understand your own motives for becoming angry, surrender those motives to Christ, and then choose to serve each other in love.

Want help with the laundry? There's nothing wrong with that. Nor is there anything wrong with the desire to have a happy marriage, have children one day, or grow in a career. But when we allow these desires to take over, we can become manipulative, resentful, and divisive—none of which bring honor to God.

Ultimately, we need to decide which desire will rule our hearts—the desire to put ourselves first and control outcomes, or the desire to make God great in our lives and live with contentment in what he *does* promise. This isn't to say there's no need to hold our spouses and families to certain standards. It's more a question of whose standards we're holding them to—our own or Christ's?

Choosing to hold ourselves and our spouses to Christ's standards rather than our own is an outward reflection of an inner resolve to let Christ's will—rather than our own—be done in our lives. This shift puts us in alignment with Christ and allows us to mature as believers as we seek out his will for our lives.

There's no doubt that it can be difficult to examine our own desires and recognize when they might be controlling our hearts or leading us into anger when we don't get what we want. But as we seek to align ourselves with Christ and his will, we can make the choice to abide by Christ's standards rather than our own. When we practice surrendering all of our desires to God, Christ will be glorified in all aspects of our lives, and we will find contentment in his promises.

Reflection

- Recall the last two or three times you became angry with your spouse. What similarities, if any, do you notice in those situations? What clues might they provide about the underlying desires that are being thwarted or that are battling within you?

- Consider the desires you have for your marriage, such as intimacy, better communication, or shared hobbies. How do you imagine your relationship might change if you prioritized these desires in a way that aligns with Christ's teachings and values?

- What desires do you find yourself holding on to tightly, even if they conflict with God's plan?

Prayer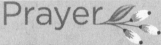

Ask God to:

- give you the ability to recognize and confront the underlying desires that lead you to become angry when you don't get what you want.

- help you align your desires with his desires for your life and marriage.

- forgive you for the times you have held on to your own desires over God's will.

- give you the strength to hold yourself and your spouse to Christ's standards rather than your own.

- provide guidance and discernment as you surrender your desires and submit your will to God's will.

DIGGING DEEPER

Cultivating the Heart

If you were having a cup of coffee with a friend, you'd probably have no trouble admitting that you sometimes act in a selfish, prideful, or angry manner, or that you place undue value on things other than Christ. Everyone struggles with these issues at different times in life, so admitting them is easy. In fact, it would be problematic if we couldn't admit to having these struggles.

However, it's easier to acknowledge these issues in general than it is to recognize them in the moments they cause hurt, anger, and disunity in our marriage. This is because we can be blinded by our emotions or unaware of how our behavior affects our partners. Therefore, it's important to reflect on those moments afterward and learn the lessons they can teach us, so we'll be better prepared to respond when similar situations arise in the future. By doing so, we can work to improve our relationships and become better partners to our spouses.

Journal Exercise: Practice Awareness

For the next seven days, take time at the beginning or end of your day to write down when you struggled with any of the four issues covered in the previous chapters—idolatry, selfishness, pride, and anger. The goal is not to beat yourself up but to become more aware of your thoughts, emotions, and behaviors in these situations. Practicing awareness will enable you to reflect on these instances in the future and take steps to realign your heart with the heart of Christ.

Moreover, this exercise will help you develop a deeper understanding of yourself and your tendencies, as well as the patterns or triggers that contribute to these negative experiences. By taking the time to observe and record your struggles, you'll be able to take a more proactive approach to personal growth and to the strengthening of your marriage.

Write your daily journal entry in four parts:

- **Triggering event.** Briefly reflect on the previous twenty-four hours—morning, afternoon, and evening. For each part of the day, consider any interactions you had with your spouse that either didn't feel right for some reason or that were clearly negative. Write down the event (words, behaviors, circumstances) that triggered the negative experience.
- **Surface behavior.** Surface behavior is your initial response—what you did and/or said in response to the triggering event.
- **Underlying issue.** Pray through each circumstance. Ask God to search your heart and reveal any underlying issues

of idolatry, selfishness, pride, or anger. Write down any insights about why you felt and reacted in the way you did.

- **A new approach.** Consider how you might approach similar situations differently in the future—with humility, grace, forgiveness, and love. Imagine being aligned with Christ as you interact with your spouse.

For example:

- **Triggering event:** *My husband left this morning without taking out the trash.*
- **Surface behavior:** *I immediately texted him, asking why the trash was left for me when he knew I had a busy morning.*
- **Underlying issue:** *I reacted in anger. And I also assumed the worst of my husband, thinking that he selfishly left the chore for me.*
- **A new approach:** *One way I can work to improve this situation is to assume the best of my spouse rather than assuming he doesn't care about me. I can ask God to help him be more attentive to my needs and his household responsibilities. I can have a conversation with him about why it matters to me that he remembers to take out the trash. Assuming the best of him, I can say, "Hey, I know you didn't mean to, but you forgot to take out the trash this morning. I didn't want it piling up over the next week, so I went ahead and gathered it and took it out to the street, but it was challenging because I was also trying to get the kids ready for school. Since this is something that keeps happening, can we think of ways to help you remember so it doesn't fall on me again on busy mornings?"*

Note that if your new approach includes talking about the issue with your spouse, prepare ahead of time by asking God to help you bring all things—your desires, your words, your attitudes, and your behaviors—into submission to Christ Jesus. Your goal in the conversation is to address the issue in a way that reflects Christ's love for you and your spouse and Christ's desire for unity.

After completing your seven journal entries, briefly review what you wrote down for each day. Make another journal entry to reflect on the following questions:

- What similarities, if any, are evident in the events that trigger a reaction in me?
- Which of the four issues—idolatry, selfishness, pride, anger—do I struggle with most? Why?
- What unhealthy or self-defeating patterns are evident in the way my spouse and I interact?
- How do I hope a new approach might help me grow personally and help my spouse and me grow together?

One thing it's important to be clear about is that it is not your sole responsibility to keep peace and harmony in your marriage. Assuming that role would lead to an extremely lopsided union of dominance and submission. Instead, you are working to improve anything and everything that is within your control to improve. You cannot change your spouse, but you can change yourself.

Accountability

After working to recognize areas of idolatry, selfishness, pride, and anger, reach out to a trusted friend for support. Ask them to hold you accountable for any changes you want to make. For example, you might start by setting up a regular meeting to talk about how you're doing in these areas. Ask them to pray for you daily between meetings, to speak truth into your life, and to encourage you as you make progress.

When seeking an accountability partner, choose someone who genuinely wants to see you grow and succeed in your relationship with Christ and in your marriage. This person should be trustworthy, nonjudgmental, and willing to speak truth into your life. In your first meeting, establish clear expectations and boundaries for the accountability relationship. This might include how often you will check in with each other, how you will communicate, and the specific areas you want to focus on.

Accountability can be a powerful tool for both personal and relational growth. When you invite another person to hold you accountable, you are taking an active role in becoming the person you want to be and cultivating the marriage you want to have.

Be the First to Change

When you want something in your marriage to change, the best place to start is with your own heart and behaviors. You may find this extremely difficult, especially if you're the first or only person willing make a change for the better. However, I encourage you to keep doing what you know is right and to ask the Lord for strength in the meantime. Even if your spouse doesn't join you at first, I'm confident they will feel the change in you before long, which may spark their desire to make a change as well. But if that's not the case, you may need additional help, such as professional counseling. Until you get to that point, continue to bring your own thoughts and actions under submission to Christ and fervently ask him to work in both your heart and the heart of your spouse.

PART 2

SHOWERING GRACE

very year when I was growing up, we attended a Christian family camp in upstate New York. Each week, the camp had a featured speaker. One week, the speaker asked all married couples to stand and then asked them to sit down based on the number of years they had been married.

"If you've been married for a year or less, please sit down," he began. One couple sat down. Then he went in five-year increments, asking couples who'd been married for five, ten, fifteen years, and so on to sit down. Eventually, only one couple was left standing. "How many years have you been married?" the speaker asked. As it turned out, they were celebrating fifty years of marriage that week.

The next question he asked of the wife surprised me. "How does he like his eggs?"

"Scrambled, with salt and pepper," she responded. She didn't even have to think.

The speaker went on to explain that after fifty years of marriage, you pretty much know everything there is to know about each other. You know how your spouse wakes up in the morning—whether they're cheerful or need to finish their coffee before they speak to anyone. You know if they're a fast driver or a slow driver, and what will make them tear up at the movies. The speaker's point that day was that God knows us even more intimately than a couple married fifty years knows each other—he knows us inside and out.

At thirteen years old, I sat there wondering if I would one day be able to answer questions about my spouse as easily as this woman had. Now, after ten years of marriage, I realize how easy that scrambled egg question is. I probably could have answered it after three months of marriage. But what I didn't realize at thirteen was that the truly impressive thing wasn't that this couple knew each other's breakfast preferences; it was the fact that they had stuck it out for fifty years *despite* knowing every little detail there was to know about each other.

Think about it. After fifty years, you've seen your spouse at their very best and their very worst. You've been through it all together. You've likely had amazing times, such as traveling together, welcoming a child into the world, or buying your first home. And you've trudged through the worst of times, such as financial instability, job loss, losing a loved one, or starting over in a new city. In addition, you've loved and suffered with each other through the inevitable day-to-day grievances of life together—the kind of irritations that create sparks of conflict in a marriage, some of which become wildfires. Things like unmet expectations, mismatched communication styles, vastly different upbringings, and even different spending and saving habits. Unless, of course, you've learned to shower everything in grace and forgiveness.

I think about this every time we visit a local state park where there's a Smokey Bear sign at the entrance. The sign includes a color-coded meter with a sweep hand that points to that day's potential fire risk—low, moderate, high, very high, extreme. During the heat of summer, the hand hovers over the red area to the right indicating an extreme risk of fire. At that point, it's been weeks without rain, the grass is dry and brittle, and even the smallest spark can set off a raging fire that will destroy the entire park. But after a heavy rainfall, the hand on the dial once again hovers over the green area to the left, indicating a low risk of fire.

A similar principle applies in marriage. Without grace, our relationships can become dry and brittle, vulnerable to even the smallest spark of frustration or conflict that comes along. However, if we continuously shower the garden of our marriage with grace, those same small sparks of frustration and conflict will simply burn out.

What does grace look like in real life? It looks like a husband who seeks to understand the deeper reason behind his wife's irritation that morning during a hectic routine of getting the kids ready for school and asks how he can help instead of returning the attitude. It looks like a wife who graciously supports her husband's latest healthy eating and exercise regimen (however long it lasts) because she understands that he wants to be the best he can be for their family. It looks like husbands and wives who go to each other and choose vulnerability by asking for grace and forgiveness for their shortcomings.

The apostle Paul wrote, "Bear with each other and forgive one another if any of you has a grievance against someone. Forgive as the Lord forgave you" (Colossians 3:13). Paul foresaw that sometimes it isn't always a huge conflict that causes pain and division. Sometimes it's the little things—the quirks, inconsistencies, and small resentments that make a relationship tinder for the smallest spark. This is why he encourages us to be ready to bear with one another and forgive each other. This ministry of showering grace protects every relationship, including marriage, from division and strife.

CHAPTER 5

Expensive Forgiveness

very household has its designated money person. Whether the responsibility is thrust on them or they take it on gladly (because the idea of someone else being in control of the budgeting is more stressful than budgeting itself), someone's got to do it. In our family, I'm the money person. And early in our marriage, things were tight. We were in our early twenties, had a six-month-old, and both worked part-time jobs while trying to balance being new parents with finishing school.

One day, I decided that getting a camera would be a great investment. I'd always loved photography, and I thought that if I took the time to learn it and practice, I could help bring in more income for our little family. The problem was, we could barely afford our rent each month, let alone a new camera that, let's be honest, was more of a want than a need at the time.

Since I was the money person, I was able to convince Josh we could afford it. I mean, technically, we could. But I also knew Josh wouldn't agree to the purchase if he knew how little we actually had in the bank.

Not long after getting the camera, Josh asked if we could make a decent-sized purchase. Assuming we had more money in the bank than we did, he thought the expense wouldn't be too much trouble but wanted to run it by me first. Cue being reminded of my guilt.

I couldn't hide it from him any longer. While I hadn't lied, per se, I definitely hadn't been fully honest. There was no way we could afford that purchase.

Josh, of course, was frustrated. And hurt.

Not only had I not been honest about our finances, but I had also manipulated him into agreeing to something that wasn't wise, and now we were in a tough spot with our finances. Not to mention that this wasn't the first time I'd done something like this. Like when we'd create a grocery list together and I'd come home with more than what we planned. Not being transparent with him about our finances and spending was a deceptive pattern. And when the truth came out, we both felt the consequences.

When we sin against someone or they sin against us, there is always a cost—a price someone has to pay. When I wasn't honest with Josh about our finances, not only did we lose money and some of our financial security, but I also lost Josh's trust. Fortunately for me, Josh chose not to hold on to his anger, and he forgave me. But that didn't mean we were suddenly able to buy what he wanted. He had to sacrifice what he wanted to pay the price for what I had done. When we're sinned against, it isn't just hurtful; it's costly.

It's costly because we've lost something or suffered harm, and it's costly because it requires that we do the work of forgiveness.

The Work of Forgiveness

In some Christian communities, "doing a Matthew 18" is shorthand for, "I need to confront someone about how they've sinned against me." That's because Matthew 18:15–17 contains Jesus' teaching about how to address sin and initiate forgiveness with another believer. It's a vital passage about the work of forgiveness, and we'll take a closer look at it shortly. But first, I want to briefly step back to get an overview of Matthew 18 as a whole. In addition to providing essential context for verses 15–17, the chapter features two parables—one that demonstrates the extent to which God longs to be reunited with us when we stray, and another about why it's so important that we learn to forgive one another.

Matthew 18 is comprised of thirty-five verses and includes a mix of teaching and storytelling about life in the kingdom. Thematically, the chapter follows this outline:

- pride (verses 1–5)
- stumbling blocks (verses 6–9)
- the Father does not wish anyone to perish (verses 10–14)
- confrontation (verses 15–20)
- mercy and forgiveness (verses 21–35)[1]

Let's take a closer look at each of these themes in Matthew 18.

---

1. I'm blown away by how this thematic outline could also be an outline of the gospel story—how God meets us in our fallen condition and saves us. It's a gospel Easter egg—a truth delightfully hidden in plain sight—that shows God's hand at work. The more I read the Bible, the more I notice how so many of its stories have gospel Easter eggs hidden within them, just waiting for us to see God's hand working and the gospel playing out in the lives of everyday people.

Pride (verses 1–5)

The chapter begins with the disciples asking Jesus, "Who, then, is the greatest in the kingdom of heaven?" (Matthew 18:1). In their pride, they likely expected Jesus to choose one of them as the greatest or to establish a hierarchy among them. This would have elevated their status on earth as followers of Jesus because of their anticipated "position" in the kingdom of heaven. The disciples sought to secure their place in the kingdom Jesus would soon establish. Therefore, they were likely surprised by Jesus' response: "Whoever takes the lowly position of [a] child is the greatest in the kingdom of heaven" (verse 4).

Stumbling Blocks (verses 6–9)

Jesus goes on to issue some stern warnings about causing others—especially those weaker than us—to stumble:

> "If anyone causes one of these little ones—those who believe in me—to stumble, it would be better for them to have a large millstone hung around their neck and to be drowned in the depths of the sea. Woe to the world because of the things that cause people to stumble! Such things must come, but woe to the person through whom they come!" (Matthew 18:6–7)

Note that while Jesus uses the term "little ones" here, Bible scholars point out that Jesus is not describing young children but rather young believers, "disciples who have stumbled off the path of discipleship because of mistreatment and temptations to sin that come through other people . . . or . . . through their own passions."[2] And the consequences Jesus describes for causing others to stumble are severe!

Similarly, when we encounter something that causes us to stumble in our own lives, Jesus says we must deal with it immediately: "If your hand or your foot causes you to stumble, cut it off and throw it away. It is better for you to enter life maimed or crippled than to have two hands or two feet and be thrown into eternal fire" (Matthew 18:8). Jesus is using hyperbole to make a point, but the point is clear: take your stumbling blocks seriously!

The good news is that Jesus knows we will stumble, that stumbling itself is inevitable. Jesus understands even better than we do that we fall into temptation of all sorts, even when we desperately want to please him with our lives. That's why he came to earth—to keep us from perishing in our sins.

The Father Does Not Wish Anyone to Perish (verses 10–14)

Jesus tells the parable of the lost sheep to demonstrate how much God loves us and wants to be reconciled with us.

> "What do you think? If a man owns a hundred sheep, and one of them wanders away, will he not leave the ninety-nine on the hills and go to look for the one that wandered off? And if he finds it, truly I tell you, he is happier about that one sheep than about the ninety-nine that did not wander off. In

---

2. Michael J. Wilkens, "The Divine Search for Lost Sheep (18:12–14)," in *The NIV Application Commentary: Matthew* (Grand Rapids: Zondervan, 2004), 617.

the same way your Father in heaven is not willing that any of these little ones should perish." (Matthew 18:12–14)

This is a picture of just how much Jesus loves us! He not only takes notice of us, but he goes out of his way to make it possible for us to have a relationship with him. Even when we stray, he longs to be reconciled with us. The apostle Peter reiterates this truth when he says, "The Lord is not slow in keeping his promise, as some understand slowness. Instead he is patient with you, *not wanting anyone to perish, but everyone to come to repentance*" (2 Peter 3:9, emphasis added).

Confrontation (verses 15–20)

Having established that we all sin and go astray, Jesus goes on to teach his disciples how to do the work of forgiveness when they are wronged:

> "If your brother or sister sins, go and point out their fault, just between the two of you. If they listen to you, you have won them over. But if they will not listen, take one or two others along, so that 'every matter may be established by the testimony of two or three witnesses.' If they still refuse to listen, tell it to the church; and if they refuse to listen even to the church, treat them as you would a pagan or a tax collector." (Matthew 18:15–17)

Since we know that someone close to us *will* stumble at one point or another, it's important that we have instructions for how to address it. And there may come a time when the brother or sister in Christ who needs to be confronted might just be your spouse. And it will also be you one day.

Mercy and Forgiveness (verses 21-35)

By far the longest section of Matthew 18 is Jesus' parable of the unforgiving debtor. Jesus tells the parable in response to Peter's question, "Lord, how many times shall I forgive my brother or sister who sins against me? Up to seven times?" Peter probably thinks seven times is generous, but Jesus says, "I tell you not seven times but seventy-seven times" (Matthew 18:21–22). Jesus then uses the parable to illustrate not only the vastness of God's forgiveness toward us but also how important it is to him that we forgive those who hurt us.

The story begins with a king who decided to collect on his debts. One man, a servant, owed him ten thousand talents, a form of currency in Jesus' day, which the NIV translates as "ten thousand bags of gold" (Matthew 18:24). When the man couldn't pay, the king ordered that the servant and his family be sold to pay the debt. But the servant begged for patience to repay the debt, and, to his amazement, the king had mercy and forgave the debt entirely. Remember, debts are costly and must be paid. Since it was impossible for the servant to pay, the king showed mercy by absorbing the loss himself.

After his debt was forgiven, the man encountered a fellow servant who owed him 100 denarii (or 100 silver coins), and he demanded repayment. The servant begged for patience and promised to repay the debt, just as he himself had begged for patience from the king. But the man refused and had his fellow servant thrown in jail until he could pay his debt.

To give you an idea of the staggering difference between the two debts, consider this. One denarius was the daily wage for a laborer. One talent was equal to 6,000 denarii. This means that the king forgave the man 60,000,000 denarii, or 60,000,000 days (more than 164,383 years) of labor—whereas the man's fellow servant had owed him 100 denarii—or 100 days of labor.

When the king's other servants saw what the man did, they were upset and told the king. Furious, the king confronted the man. "'You wicked servant,' he said, 'I canceled all that debt of yours because you begged me to. Shouldn't you have had mercy on your fellow servant just as I had on you?'" (Matthew 18:32–33). The king then threw the man in jail until he could repay his original debt.

It's a pretty intense story, right? And there are some clear takeaways:

- Our sin is a debt too big for us to ever repay God.
- God is merciful and absorbs our debt when we go to him and ask for forgiveness.
- God expects us to offer others this same forgiveness, fully understanding that they will stumble and need our forgiveness, likely on multiple occasions.
- If we don't show the same mercy we've been shown, God can lose his patience with us.

While we can't ignore the fact that God takes seriously our responsibility to forgive others, neither should we ignore the fact that this is because he takes his forgiveness of us seriously too. Remember how much the first servant was forgiven. Jesus told the parable to remind us that God is ready and willing to forgive us, no matter how great our debt.

Jesus doesn't sugarcoat the fact that forgiving others is costly. He gets it—more than anyone. And he unapologetically asks us to do the same. Like the servant in the parable, he expects us to forgive because we have been forgiven of so much already. In fact, if we truly grasp the depth of what Jesus has forgiven us, the forgiveness we offer to others should feel small—like it's the least we can do after everything Jesus did for us.

And even if all of that weren't enough, there's another reason we should be eager to do the work of forgiveness—that it keeps the pain of evil and hurt from spreading and doing more damage in our lives.

The Forgiveness Journal

Forgiveness is a crucial aspect in any marriage, but especially so in Christian marriage. The goals of this exercise are to deepen your understanding of how you and your spouse view forgiveness, as well as to promote unity by giving you an opportunity to practice forgiveness. First, you'll both do some individual reflection by writing in a journal, and then you'll have a conversation to discuss what you wrote.

Individual Reflection

Use a journal to reflect on the following questions:

1. How would you define forgiveness? What does forgiveness mean to you?
2. What experiences of *offering* forgiveness (to your spouse or to others) have been most meaningful to you? What experiences of *receiving* forgiveness (from your spouse or others) have been most meaningful to you?

3. What are one or two examples of times you've navigated forgiveness well in your marriage? What are one or two times you've failed to navigate forgiveness well in your marriage?

4. Identify one issue for which you need to ask your spouse's forgiveness.
   - What did you do, and why did you do it?
   - What harm did your action cause, or why was it wrong?
   - Why do you regret what you did?
   - What will you do differently in similar situations in the future?

Conversation

Find a quiet space where you and your spouse can sit comfortably and talk without distractions. Start with a short prayer, asking God to guide you, to increase your understanding of one another, and to open your hearts to forgiveness.

1. **Share insights.** Take turns sharing what you wrote about your definition of forgiveness, what forgiveness means to you, and your experiences of giving and receiving forgiveness. Listen attentively and without judgment as your partner shares. It's okay if your perspectives on forgiveness differ.

2. **Share lessons learned.** Briefly share the examples of when you did and did not navigate forgiveness well in your marriage. What lessons did you learn about forgiveness from these experiences?

3. **Request and offer forgiveness.** Take turns requesting and offering forgiveness for the situation you identified in your journal.
   - When you are requesting forgiveness begin by saying, "I'm sorry for . . ." and then acknowledge what you did. Explain why you did it but refrain from making excuses. Express your regrets and how you want to respond differently in the future.
   - When you are offering forgiveness, you might begin by saying, "I appreciate you acknowledging that. I love you, and I forgive you."
4. **Discuss strategies for future forgiveness.** Have a conversation about how you can improve your practice of forgiveness within your marriage. Share ideas on how you can both handle conflicts and disagreements in a way that promotes forgiveness and reconciliation.
5. **Close in prayer.** Pray together, thanking God for the opportunity to strengthen your marriage through forgiveness and asking for his continued guidance.

Forgiveness Stops the Spread of Evil and Hurt

Have you ever witnessed a mudslide or seen a video of one? Once a mudslide starts, it's impossible to stop. It flows fast and takes out everything in its path—roads, houses, and even whole communities. One of the main strategies used to prevent mudslides is to build ravines or channels that enable the mud to be redirected or swallowed up. And those channels are a pretty good metaphor for forgiveness. Think of it this way: If evil and hurt were a mudslide running downhill, forgiveness is the channel that diverts the destructive flow and keeps it from doing even more damage. Forgiveness saves everything that would otherwise have been taken out in its path. In that sense, forgiveness has the power to stop the spread of evil, division, and hurt—but only when we forgive in the way Jesus taught us and modeled for us.

Following Jesus' example of forgiveness is challenging for many of us because what Jesus taught and modeled about forgiveness includes some things that make us uncomfortable. For example, Jesus told his disciples, "If your brother or sister sins against you, rebuke them; and if they repent, forgive them. Even if they sin against you seven times in a day and seven times come back to you saying 'I repent,' you must forgive them" (Luke 17:3–4).

Just as we saw in Matthew 18:15–17, the work of forgiveness requires some form of confrontation or rebuke. However, if we choose to confront the sin without making peace with the other person through forgiveness, we're like the servant in the parable who demanded payment but withheld mercy. We are trying to make the other person pay the consequences for their actions while disregarding the fact that Christ has already paid the consequences for *our* actions.

When we choose to forgive, we know deep down that we can never truly get back what sin has cost us. We don't easily forget or recover from hurtful words, broken trust, or selfish actions. But sometimes it's tempting to rebuke a person and withhold forgiveness because it gives us the illusion of power—that we *can* make up for what we lost by making the other person suffer the consequences we set. However, when that happens, we're not practicing rebuke that leads to forgiveness, but rather revenge that leads to payback.

On the other hand, some of us feel uncomfortable with the rebuke part and try to skip straight to forgiveness. We want to make peace without confronting how the other person sinned against us. I'm often guilty of this, saying things like, "It's not a big deal," or "I'm already over it." However, trying to forgive without confronting the issue isn't true forgiveness; it's selfishly seeking peace for ourselves. Whatever the reason—whether the thought of confrontation makes us break out in a cold sweat, we want to be liked, or the sin is just uncomfortable to talk about—sweeping sin under the rug diminishes how hurtful and costly confrontation really is. Instead, we need to do the *complete* work of forgiveness, which requires confronting the hurt to keep it from spreading *and* seeking to make peace by offering forgiveness.

If you're anything like me, I can guess what you might be thinking right now. *That kind of forgiveness, the kind that tries to correct and make peace, sounds really, really hard.* Especially when, in Luke 17:3–4, Jesus mentions forgiving someone who sins against you seven times in one day—not to mention his response to Peter in Matthew 18 that we must forgive seventy-seven times! And it's not hard to imagine that the relationships in which we'd most likely need to forgive someone seven times in one day are marriage and parenting. That's where we'll have to do the work of forgiveness most.

Here's what gives me hope when forgiveness feels hard or even impossible. Right after Jesus tells the disciples they need to forgive someone seven times a day, their response is, "Increase our faith!" (Luke 17:5). They, too, thought this kind of forgiveness sounded overwhelming. They knew just how hard it would be to carry out the kind of forgiveness Jesus asks of us—to forgive even though it's costly and even when we're likely to be sinned against repeatedly.

But Jesus compassionately reassures his disciples, reminding them that God has the power to multiply even the smallest amount of faith: "If you have faith as small as a mustard seed, you can say to this mulberry tree, 'Be uprooted and planted in the sea,' and it will obey you" (Luke 17:6). The promise in Jesus' statement is that he can use our faith, no matter how small, to do what seems impossible—even when what seems impossible is the work of forgiveness.

If we truly understand the depth of Jesus' forgiveness for us, it should put our obligation to forgive others, particularly our spouses, into perspective. It's the least we can do for our spouses given what Jesus has done for us. Jesus humbled himself and took on our debt when he forgave us. When a spouse wrongs us, they take something from us. Forgiveness is about accepting that debt and choosing to pay it off, not just sweeping it under the rug or seeking repayment. It's about addressing the wrong and making peace instead of punishing the other person or selfishly seeking peace for ourselves. Forgiveness has nothing to do with the other person's performance. It's an action that stops the spread of evil and hurt, and it requires humility and a constant recognition of our own need for grace.

In the sacred bond of marriage, the importance of continual forgiveness cannot be overstated. Just as Jesus constantly extends his boundless forgiveness to us, we must strive to do the same for our spouses and others. Mistakes and misunderstandings are inevitable in any close relationship, but when we choose to forgive repeatedly, we demonstrate our commitment to our spouses in the same way Jesus demonstrates his unwavering commitment to us. It's a continuous act of humility, acknowledging that we, too, are imperfect beings in need of grace. Forgiveness not only mends wounds but also fortifies the foundation of trust and love on which a marriage is built. By extending forgiveness continually, we cultivate a relationship in which growth, understanding, and enduring love can flourish, ultimately strengthening the God-glorifying bond between spouses.

Reflection

- Think about a time when you were hurt by your spouse's actions or words. How did you handle the situation? Did you confront them, or did you sweep it under the rug? What was the outcome?

- Forgiveness is costly, but so is unforgiveness. What have both forgiveness and unforgiveness cost you in your relationship with your spouse?

- Consider the parable of the unforgiving debtor. How does the king's mercy and grace toward his debtor challenge you about your own willingness to forgive?

- Reflect on Jesus' teaching in Matthew 18:15–17 about confronting sin and initiating forgiveness. How can you apply these principles in your own life and relationships? What fears or challenges might you face in doing so?

- Take a moment to meditate on Ephesians 4:32: "Be kind and compassionate to one another, forgiving each other, just as in Christ God forgave you." How does this verse shape your understanding of forgiveness and its importance in your marriage?

Prayer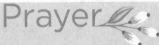

Ask God to:

- help you recognize any patterns of deception or dishonesty in your marriage and give you the courage to address them and seek forgiveness.

- give you a spirit of love for and compassion toward your spouse, even when they hurt you or disappoint you.

- help you let go of grudges and past hurts and give you the strength to forgive your spouse as Christ has forgiven you.

- allow for greater communication and understanding in your marriage so you can work with your spouse to address any issues that arise.

- guide you and your spouse in the work of forgiveness and give both of you grace to navigate conflict with humility, wisdom, and compassion.

CHAPTER 6

To Know and Be Known

It was Monday morning, and Josh and I had just driven to the gym after dropping off the kids at school. It was 25 degrees outside, and we were sitting in the car savoring the last sips of coffee in our to-go cups before braving the thirty-second dash to the gym doors. Hey, in South Carolina, 25 degrees is pretty cold! Despite the cold, I had an optimistic feeling that we were going to have a great start to our week and that it would be a productive day.

Just before stepping out of the car, Josh turned to me and said, "I want to talk to you about something."

In that moment, the optimistic feeling I'd had began to slip away from me in slow motion, kind of like when your phone begins slipping out of your hand and heading toward the floor, and there's no way to stop it.

Maybe what he has to say won't be so bad, I thought.

"About what?" I asked hesitantly.

He went on to tell me about a few things he had been notic-ing in my attitude recently and how it had affected the rest of the family. "I know you have a lot going on right now," Josh said, "but oftentimes, we can just feel the tension when you walk into the room."

I was silent for a few minutes, listening to Josh fill me in on what it had been like to live with me the past few weeks. Instead of trying to take in what he was saying, I was waiting for my moment to say something, and the defensive responses were careening around through my head, dying to be heard.

It wasn't that I took issue with anything he said. In fact, I could remember the examples he brought up and could see how my attitude had impacted my family. But I was embarrassed and ashamed that I hadn't recognized and corrected the behavior myself, and I was frustrated that Josh felt the need to call it out. So the responses flying around in my head weren't denials so much as they were justifications. Maybe if he understood why I'd been acting that way or how he was part of the problem, he would lay off a little bit.

"Well, the reason I was frustrated with David was because . . ."

"It doesn't seem fair that you're talking to me about this when you . . ."

"I've been under a lot of pressure lately . . ."

"If you had just helped me more with . . ."

And my list went on. If I could convince him that he was part of the reason for my bad attitude, I wouldn't have to feel so much shame for letting it fester in the first place. It might even keep him from confronting me about issues like this in the future.

In my shame, I pushed Josh away, afraid of allowing him to see the inner parts of me that I, myself, hated. Even after almost ten years of marriage, I hated the idea of him seeing the personal struggles I was ashamed of in myself.

Looking back, I'd like to imagine an alternate ending to this story—one in which I allow him to speak truth and wisdom into my life rather than working so hard to put up my defenses. It might have gone something like this.

"I know you have a lot going on right now," Josh said, "but often-times, we can just feel the tension when you walk into the room."

I continued to listen, feeling my defensiveness start to well up, but also working to keep an open mind. I reminded myself that Josh loved me and that he wouldn't be bringing this up—especially right now—if he didn't feel it was important. I also noticed his gentle demeanor and thought about how careful he was to be honest with me without hurting my feelings. I was grateful for that.

I thought about what he was saying before I responded, and I realized he was right. I could recall all the examples of my poor attitude. I decided to be vulnerable with him.

"I can see what you're saying," I admitted quietly. "I have had a bad attitude recently. And yeah, I do have a lot going on, but I'm sorry I've been taking that stress out on you and our family. I wouldn't want to be around that either."

"I hate that you're feeling stressed, and I want to do more to take some responsibilities off your plate," Josh offered. "I also want to take some time to pray with you. Would it be okay if we did that before we work out today?"

In that moment, my anger melted, and before we prayed together, I breathed a silent prayer of gratitude. I thanked God for knowing me inside and out and still choosing to love me, and I thanked him for a husband who was doing his best to model God's love to me.

I wish this alternate ending had been the real one. In the moment, I was so caught up in justifying myself and trying to appear perfect that I forgot a fundamental truth. It's vulnerability, not the facade of perfection, that builds connection and intimacy in marriage.

Our Short-Lived Perfection

When I think about perfection in marriage, I sometimes wonder what it was like for Adam and Eve before the fall. They are the only human beings who ever had a perfect relationship. Here's how the Bible describes it: "Therefore a man shall leave his father and his mother and hold fast to his wife, and they shall become one flesh. And the man and his wife were both naked and were not ashamed" (Genesis 2:24–25 ESV).

What did that level of vulnerability look like in real life? Unfortunately, we don't know because it wasn't long before sin entered the picture. That's when the walls of defensiveness went up and perfect vulnerability vanished. Here's how it all went wrong:

> So when the woman saw that the tree was good for food, and that it was a delight to the eyes, and that the tree was to be desired to make one wise, she took of its fruit and ate, and she also gave some to her husband who was with her, and he ate. Then the eyes of both were opened, and they knew that they were naked. And they sewed fig leaves together and made themselves loincloths.
>
> And they heard the sound of the LORD God walking in the garden in the cool of the day, and the man and his wife hid themselves from the presence of the LORD God among the trees of the garden. But the LORD God called to the man

and said to him, "Where are you?" And he said, "I heard the sound of you in the garden, and I was afraid, because I was naked, and I hid myself." He said, "Who told you that you were naked? Have you eaten of the tree of which I commanded you not to eat?" The man said, "The woman whom you gave to be with me, she gave me fruit of the tree, and I ate." Then the LORD God said to the woman, "What is this that you have done?" The woman said, "The serpent deceived me, and I ate." (Genesis 3:6–13 ESV)

Wow. We don't know how much time passed between Genesis 2 and Genesis 3, but we can see the stark difference the fall made in Adam and Eve's relationship. In the first passage, Adam and Eve are united—one flesh—and even though they were completely naked, they felt no shame. Why is that? Well, since this part of the story took place before the fall, we can assume that everything in the Garden of Eden, Adam and Eve included, was perfect and just as God intended it to be. Imagine that—having a perfect body formed by the hands of God before any imperfection had ever entered the world. Sounds pretty freeing if you ask me.

But I don't think it was having fitness influencer bodies that made it possible for the first couple to run around unashamedly naked while #livingtheirbestlife. Adam and Eve felt perfectly comfortable with being completely vulnerable—in other words, free from shame—because there simply wasn't anything to be ashamed of. Neither of them knew what it was to be selfish, to be sinful, to be untrustworthy, or to think any of those flaws might be true about their spouse.

Now let's zoom in on the second passage. We see a big

change in Adam and Eve's relationship immediately after they sinned against God. But even though they disobeyed God, did that mean there also had to be shame in the relationship they had with each other? Couldn't they go on living together—naked, vulnerable, and unashamed—despite a moment of weakness and doubt in God? Why did anything in their marriage relationship have to change after the fall?

In his book *This Momentary Marriage*, author John Piper points to two things that corrupted Adam and Eve's relationship. He notes that we feel shame in marriage today for the same reasons: "In the first case, the person viewing my nakedness is no longer trustworthy, so I am afraid I will be shamed. In the second, I myself am no longer at peace with God, and I feel guilty and defiled and unworthy—I deserve to be shamed."[1]

In other words, Adam and Eve still had the same perfect bodies they'd had before the fall, and they hadn't done anything to intentionally hurt or shame the other person. Nevertheless, their relationship could never again be what it was before sin entered the world.

Sin created a divide between what should have been and what was. Living in a shame-free, guilt-free, completely vulnerable and trusting relationship was now a thing of the past. Because Adam and Eve understood that they were each capable of sin, shame was now a part of their relationship, and their perfect vulnerability with each other quickly vanished. Adam realized that if Eve was capable of sin, she could no longer be fully trusted to love him perfectly because she was selfish and

---

1. John Piper, *This Momentary Marriage: A Parable of Permanence* (Wheaton, IL: Crossway, 2009), 35.

would put her desires first. And because Adam was sinful, he no longer felt worthy of Eve's complete trust and unconditional love.

Shame and insecurity were the logical consequences of both realizations. And once shame was on the scene, Adam and Eve's new distrust of each other caused them to hide, cover themselves, and even to deflect blame in defense of their own failures—Adam blamed Eve, and Eve blamed the serpent.

Sin Causes Us to Hide

Why do we hide by attempting to downplay, deflect, or cover up our sin? Because we're afraid of what we may lose if the truth became known. When Josh confronted me about my shortcomings, I tried to give every excuse for why he should understand them and allow them. I even tried to make them partly his fault. If I brought him down to my level, there'd be less to judge, right?

But the truth is, I was selfishly and fearfully covering my sin out of fear of being vulnerable and unlovable. I was afraid of losing Josh's respect and maybe even causing severe damage to our relationship. Why would Josh want to be married to someone with a sour attitude? I was embarrassed at the very least and scared at the very most. In the same way, Adam's and Eve's effort to clothe themselves was a sinful effort to conceal what they had done from God.

When God asked Adam and Eve where they were in the garden, they hid because their nakedness left them feeling exposed and vulnerable. And yet God didn't tell them that their sin was too much for him or that they were too far gone. Instead, he showed them mercy by creating coverings that were far superior to anything they could have made for themselves: "The LORD

God made clothing from animal skins for Adam and his wife" (Genesis 3:21 NLT). Note that their covering didn't come without sacrifice—animals were slain so they could be clothed. Even though God is ready and waiting to offer us forgiveness, that doesn't mean there aren't consequences for our sin.

Just as Adam and Eve's sin had real consequences, my sin had consequences too. And I wasn't the only one who had to bear them. Josh felt the pain of my negative attitude and then had to do the work of forgiveness. When he confronted me about it, he wasn't seeking punishment or retribution. Instead, he covered the situation in grace and gently asked for repentance and reconciliation. He was doing the work of forgiveness to redeem what I had done and to restore our relationship.

My initial reaction was to hide. I felt too exposed and vulnerable in my weakness, and I was embarrassed that he saw my sin. But what I've learned is that Christ (and those who love me as Christ does) will meet me exactly where I am, invite me to come out of hiding, and seek out a redemptive relationship with me—a relationship that doesn't allow me to stay in my sin, but one that sees it for what it is and calls me out of it and into Christ's open arms of grace.

Redemption is the act of God's grace and mercy through which we, and all of humanity, are saved from the consequences of sin and restored to a right relationship with God. Through his death on the cross, we're offered forgiveness, reconciliation with God, and the hope of eternal life. Redemption is the example God set for us the very moment sin entered the world, and it was his design for marriage from the beginning—that it be a redeeming covenant relationship symbolizing God's relationship with his people.

As disheartening as Adam and Eve's story sounds when

taken at face value—you know, having a perfect relationship with the creator of the universe, living in a perfect world, being perfect, and then losing it all—God uses what happens after the fall to foreshadow not only the ultimate redemption to come in Christ but also the redemption we can experience within marriage. While Adam and Eve never had to practice forgiveness and reconciliation before the fall, marriage was always designed with those practices in mind. God didn't have to remodel marriage after the fall; it was already fit to be a picture of God's promise to us. He designed marriage to be a covenant of love that doesn't break in the face of our sinful nature but rather works to redeem it and bring glory to the one who designed marriage.

Rejuvenating Redemption

At this point in your marriage, you've probably been confronted by your spouse in one way or another. They may have done it with a humble heart in hopes of reconciliation, or they may have done it in anger (which, I would argue, can be another opportunity to show grace). Whatever the case, we can find so much comfort and joy in the fact that marriage is designed to be redeeming. And yet we can't be redeemed without also being called to holiness, either when were convicted in our hearts that we have done wrong or when God uses our spouses to call us to repentance and reconciliation.

With the understanding that God can and often does work through our spouses to open our eyes to our own sin and call us back to himself, we can make the choice to be vulnerable—to tear down our defensive walls when our spouses bravely speak the truth in love. And it goes without saying that such vulnerability is a two-way street. In a marriage of two human beings with sinful natures, both need redemption and reconciliation. If you feel as though you are the only one who is expected to be vulnerable and asked to change your attitudes or behaviors in your relationship, that's a red flag—and perhaps an indication that counseling or some other form of support or intervention may be needed.

Pursuing holiness and redemption means Christian spouses ought to be able to foster a mutual vulnerability that casts out shame in marriage. That's the kind of vulnerability that diligently addresses sin, humbly admits sin, seeks forgiveness, and rejoices in reconciliation—over and over again. That kind of vulnerability is an expression of the love the apostle John described when he wrote, "Such love has no fear, because perfect love expels all fear. If we are afraid, it is for fear of punishment, and this shows that we have not fully experienced his perfect love" (1 John 4:18 NLT).

When we commit to practicing redemption in marriage, we no longer need to put effort into trying to hide our sin and shame. Instead, we can choose openness and honesty with our spouses, allowing ourselves to be vulnerable without fear of being fully known or exposed. We can come to our spouses with humility, owning our mistakes and seeking forgiveness and redemption together. Of course, this can be difficult since it requires putting aside our pride. But if we're increasingly willing to do so, we'll have more confidence in our relationship, knowing that we are working together to make Christ's love more richly experienced. Plus, we'll make room for a healthier and more honest relationship in which we can be fully ourselves and more trusting of each other.

God designed marriage to function with this redeeming love from the very beginning because it's what brings him the most glory. And our willingness to live out this love in marriage continuously points to Christ, God's ultimate and permanent solution to the problem of our shame.

When we know we are secure in covenant love—with both God and our spouses—we can be transparent about our sin, bring it out into the open, and ask for forgiveness. When we do this in marriage, we actively work together toward holiness, striving for the relationship Adam and Eve enjoyed with each other and with God before the fall. And we can continue to work in grace toward refining this redeeming relationship until Christ returns and makes all things new again.

Reflection

- Briefly recall the last two or three times you were confronted by your spouse. How did you react? What thoughts or emotions motivated your reactions when you were confronted?

- Briefly recall the last two or three times you confronted your spouse. How would you describe your motives in doing so? For example, would you say you were motivated more by seeking revenge and retribution or by seeking reconciliation and redemption? Why?

- In what ways, if any, could the situations you just recalled have been different if you or your spouse had chosen to respond differently—to be vulnerable or not to be vulnerable?

- In what areas of your marriage do you wish you had more vulnerability and less defensiveness? If you could experience the kind of redemption this chapter describes, how do you imagine your marriage might be different?

Prayer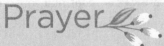

Ask God to:

- reveal areas of sin and shame in your life and in your marriage and give you the desire to confess and seek forgiveness.

- give you courage to be vulnerable with your spouse, even when it's difficult or uncomfortable.

- lower your defenses, giving you the ability to listen to your spouse's critiques with an open mind and a loving heart.

- supply patience and grace as you and your spouse work together toward holiness and a stronger relationship.

CHAPTER 7

The Mystery of Marriage

"Evy finally went to sleep," I said to Josh as I got to the top of the stairs on the third floor of his parents' home—which served as our bedroom, closet, living area, and home office. "Oh, and your mom asked if you would mow the lawn tomorrow," I said as I plopped down on the couch.

"I just mowed a few days ago, but okay," Josh said as he turned off his computer and came to join me on the couch.

"Look at this house I found," I said, handing him my phone, which was open to the Realtor.com app.

"Yeah, that's nice," he nodded.

"It's in our price range," I continued, taking back my phone and scrolling through the photos.

Sensing my disappointment, he said, "Chels, you know there's not really any point in looking right now. We're not ready." He tried to make eye contact, but I avoided his gaze.

"We've been here a year and a half, Josh," I sighed.

"I know, Chels," he said gently, "but that doesn't change anything. I've gone over the numbers with you. If we bought that house today and put down what we have saved, we won't be able to make that mortgage payment work. We need to wait."

I knew he was right, but that didn't make me any less sad. That night, like many others, I scrolled through pictures of houses we couldn't yet afford, dreaming of the life I hoped to give our family one day. At the time, I'm glad I didn't know it would be almost another year until we moved into our home. The saving and paying off debt that I thought would take only six to twelve months ended up taking almost three years.

During that time, we continuously worked toward our goal, paying off debt and saving for a down payment. Josh was the one who calculated how much we could afford, the neighborhoods where we should house-hunt, the best schools, and proximity to grocery stores, the gym, and downtown. He even calculated the percentage of sunshine we could expect to have each year, which was a big deal at the time since we lived in rainy Washington State. Then, when the time finally came, he did a great job negotiating our mortgage rate to make sure our payments fell well within our budget. By the time we bought our home, we had $0.00 in credit card debt.

We've been in the home we bought in South Carolina ever since, and I can't imagine living anywhere else. Our kids play safely in our neighborhood with tons of neighbor friends, we love their school, and our home is affordable yet big enough to host children in foster care or our families when they visit from out of town.

If I had gotten my way, we would have bought a house and moved years before we were truly ready. And although it was admittedly very hard for me to submit to Josh's leadership at the time, I truly believe God blessed Josh's servant leadership and my submission to him to provide a home even better than we imagined.

As I come to understand that marriage is designed to be a picture of Christ and his church, I also understand that the more my spouse and I relate to one another as Christ and the church do, the better our relationship functions.

Christlikeness over Compatibility

In college, two of our best friends started dating. Adeline came from a family of all girls, and Nicholas came from a family of all boys. In the beginning of their relationship, Adeline commented that she liked how Nicholas couldn't care less about what he wore. He typically wore a tracksuit with matching colors for the pants and jacket or a large T-shirt tucked into basketball shorts. To her, not being superficial about what he wore was a great quality. And she's right—it is!

But I also remember laughing with Adeline when, about a year into their marriage, she complained how difficult it was to get Nicholas to care about what he wore, to not wear the same raggedy pants all the time, and how she had to do all his shopping for him. It hadn't taken long for what she once considered a cute, positive quirk to turn into a point of minor frustration.

As much as we like to think we can find our perfect match, no two human beings fit together like perfect puzzle pieces. If you've been married for any amount of time, you already know this. But the Bible has a much higher calling for marriage than mere compatibility anyway.

In the book of Genesis, God says the man and the woman are to be joined together and no longer be two separate entities, but one (Genesis 2:24). Jesus reiterated this and quoted the Genesis verse when he said, "'For this reason a man shall leave his father and mother and be joined to his wife, and the two shall become one flesh'; so then they are no longer two, but one flesh. Therefore what God has joined together, let not man separate" (Mark 10:7–9 NKJV).

The apostle Paul quotes the same Genesis verse in his letter to the church at Ephesus and adds, "This mystery is profound, and I am saying that it refers to Christ and the church" (Ephesians 5:32 ESV). Paul is pointing to the mystery of two individuals becoming united into one. It's a supernatural bond designed to represent to the rest of the world the unique relationship Christ has with his church. That's a huge responsibility!

This bond is also part of what makes marriage so important. Marriage is about more than just having a more fulfilling, happy, and stable life; it's about being a tangible illustration—to both believers and unbelievers—of how Christ loves the church. Let that sink in for a minute. Marriage has a higher purpose—one we can't take lightly. And in this light, we must ask the question, "How exactly does marriage represent Christ to the world?"

Three Ways Marriage Represents Christ to the World

I believe there are three unique ways marriage represents Christ to the world, and you'll find they are curiously similar to the mission Christ had while he was on earth. Christian marriage is radically forgiving, redemptive, and makes us holier.

Christian Marriage Is Radically Forgiving

Our first opportunity to show Christ to the world, and one that will happen most often, is the practice of radical forgiveness.

Couples in even the happiest marriages must learn to practice forgiveness. This includes digging deep to forgive big things, such as betrayal, but it also includes developing stamina to forgive the many small, daily grievances that clutter a relationship. Over time, a spouse's shortcomings can be like the slow, maddening drip of a faucet causing us to become resentful and bitter. Have you ever asked your spouse to lock the back door before they go to bed at night? Have you ever asked them a thousand times? Then you understand what I mean.

In his letter to the church at Colossae, Paul gives this practical advice on how believers should love one another other: "Bear with each other and forgive one another if any of you has a grievance against someone. Forgive as the Lord forgave you. And over all these virtues put on love, which binds them all together in perfect unity" (Colossians 3:13–14).

Rapidly forgiving the little things is one way to bear with one another. That's more important than it might seem because it's the small cracks of division—unmet expectations, a hurtful word said in anger, personality differences, or even plain forgetfulness—that can eventually lead to large divides. By bearing with one another, we exemplify the same love Christ has for us, bearing with one another's human inadequacies and offering forgiveness again and again.

Christian Marriage Is Redemptive

In the context of God's Word, redemption is the act of God's deliverance of his people from the chains of sin and its consequences. Redemption pulls us out of darkness, which is something we could never do for ourselves. Likewise, in marriage, we have the unique opportunity to take an honest look at our spouse—to see them for everything they are—and then, in love, appeal to them to come closer to Christ in both their desires and actions.

There may be no one else in the world who knows the sins your spouse struggles with as well as you do. Similarly, your spouse may be the only one who knows the sins you're prone to. This gives both of you the opportunity and responsibility to be Christ to one another in the ways you call each other out of sin and into service. And because of this, God can use both of you to bring the other into a closer relationship with Christ.

Christian Marriage Makes Us Holier

In a similar way, a godly marriage relationship acts as a whetstone, the relational equivalent of a tool that keeps swords and other tools sharp. As the book of Proverbs declares, "As iron sharpens iron, so one person sharpens another" (Proverbs 27:17). In other words, through their interactions and companionship, husbands and wives can challenge, encourage, and strengthen one another, just as iron sharpens iron.

This idea that marriage makes us holier is vastly different from what the world believes a relationship should be. The perspective of the world is, "If you call me out on my shortcomings or sin, you are judgmental and closed-minded. If you think I can improve, you're not accepting me for who I am. If I have to forgive you repeatedly, I'm settling for less than I deserve."

Part of what makes Christian marriage so different is that we are called to put our primary focus not on ourselves but on our spouses. We do this not because we are less important than our spouses, but because, like Christ, we are called to model sacrificial submission to each other. When our culture says, "Love yourself," Jesus says, "Deny yourself" (Matthew 16:24).

Mutual Submission

In Ephesians 5, when Paul quotes Genesis 2:24—that "the two shall become one flesh"—he draws a parallel between the roles of husbands and wives in marriage and the distinctive roles of Christ and the church. This means that husbands and wives can learn how to love one another by modeling their relationship on what God intended for Christ and the church.

Paul begins by stating the foundational principle of Christian marriage: "Submit to one another out of reverence for Christ" (Ephesians 5:21). Such mutual submission means we serve each other and prioritize our spouse's needs. Paul then goes on to describe what submission looks like for both husbands and wives and how that submission reflects the relationship between Christ and the church.

> Wives, submit yourselves to your own husbands as you do to the Lord. For the husband is the head of the wife as Christ is the head of the church, his body, of which he is the Savior. Now as the church submits to Christ, so also wives should submit to their husbands in everything.
>
> Husbands, love your wives, just as Christ loved the church and gave himself up for her to make her holy, cleansing her by the washing with water through the word, and to present her to himself as a radiant church, without stain or wrinkle or any other blemish, but holy and blameless. (Ephesians 5:22–27)

Wives can follow the church's example and be subject to their husbands, while husbands love their wives as Christ loved the church and lead with sacrificial love. The husband's role is to lead with a love that's willing to die in order that the wife may live, while the wife's role is to be inclined to yield to her husband's authority and follow his leadership, but never to follow him into sin.

I use the phrase "inclined to yield" to describe a *willingness* to yield and a *tendency* to follow, because we're never asked to blindly follow another human. A husband never replaces Christ as a supreme authority, and wives are never expected to follow their husbands into sin. However, even when a Christian wife does have to make the decision to stand with Christ against her husband's sinful will, she can still demonstrate a spirit of submission. She can show, through her attitudes and actions, that she doesn't enjoy resisting her husband's will and that she hopes for him to leave his sin behind and lead in righteousness. This way, her disposition is to honor him, and his leadership can once again be in alignment with Christ.

Wives take their unique cues in marriage from the church's submission to Christ, and husbands take their unique cues from Christ's love for the church. Paul begins his instructions for husbands by establishing the foundation of love: "Husbands, love your wives, as Christ loved the church and gave himself up for her" (Ephesians 5:25). Husbands are to lead with the kind of sacrificial love that is willing to die so that the wife may live. As Jesus says, "The one who rules [should become] like the one who serves" (Luke 22:26).

Christ himself exemplified this love for us. He loved the church so much that he gave himself up for her. So when Paul speaks of a husband's role, he's not envisioning a dictator, but rather a servant leader. The husband must lead with humility and be willing to put the needs of his wife before his own. Going even further, Paul writes, "In this same way, husbands ought to love their wives as their own bodies. He who loves his wife loves himself. After all, no one ever hated their own body, but they feed and care for their body, just as Christ does the church" (Ephesians 5:28–29).

In speaking to husbands, Paul affirms the unique oneness of marriage, pointing out that to love one's spouse is to love oneself. It's obvious that if you don't care for your own body, you're going to be much less effective in other areas of your life. Therefore taking care of your body is a top priority. Here Paul is saying that husbands must prioritize their wives above everything else, as if they were prioritizing their own health.

Sadly, since humanity's fall recorded in Genesis, we often see the harmony of marriage cracked by the twisting of a husband's loving headship into either unloving domination or passive indifference, and the twisting of a wife's intelligent, willing submission into either manipulation or blatant disregard. But through the grace of God, Christian couples can still reflect a picture of Christ's relationship to the church, one that showcases God's love to the world. Wives can live out true submission by following the example of God's intention for the church, and husbands can live out true headship by modeling their leadership after Christ's loving service to the church. In doing this, couples radically prioritize each other over themselves, setting themselves apart from the "me first" values of our culture and displaying Christ's beautiful plan to redeem his people.

Jesus Prayed for Our Unity

Near the end of his earthly ministry, Jesus prayed for his disciples and for all who would come to believe in him.

> My prayer is not for [my disciples] alone. I pray also for those who will believe in me through their message, that all of them may be one, Father, just as you are in me and I am in you. May they also be in us so that the world may believe that you have sent me. I have given them the glory that you gave me, that they may be one as we are one—I in them and you in me—so that they may be brought to complete unity. Then the world will know that you sent me and have loved me. (John 17:20–23)

I find it interesting that Jesus prayed for complete unity but not for uniformity. In other words, he didn't ask God to make his followers completely compatible with one another or to make everyone like each other more. Nor did he ask God to make his followers work together more efficiently, using their complementary skills. Instead, he asked God for unity among his followers because it would show the world that he, Jesus, is indeed our Savior.

Just as the Father, the Son, and the Holy Spirit are one—just as Christ and his church are one—husbands and wives are also one. When the world says, "Me," God says, "No. *Them.*" In this unity, marriage can be a testimony—to believers and nonbelievers alike—of Christ's desire for oneness with us and can act as a beacon of forgiveness, redemption, and holiness to the world.

Reflection

- Briefly recall a time when you prioritized your spouse's needs above your own. What did that decision require of you? Now recall a time when your spouse prioritized your needs above their own. How did your spouse model sacrificial love? How did the choices both you and your spouse made impact your relationship?

- Christian marriage represents Christ to the world through *radical forgiveness*, a *redemptive mindset*, and *growth in holiness*.
  - Which of these three have you experienced most in your marriage? Which would you like to experience more?
  - How would you characterize the practice of forgiveness in your marriage? For example, is forgiveness readily or grudgingly given? Is forgiveness superficial or radical?
  - In what areas of your character or behavior do you wish your spouse would sharpen you by encouraging you to become the best version of yourself?

- What are some small grievances in your marriage— the kind of daily irritations that could become sources of resentment for both you and your spouse? In what ways, if any, do you already choose to forgive and bear with each other in love?

How has choosing to bear with, or not to bear with, impacted your ability to forgive one another?

- Allow yourself to dream a little about how you hope you and your spouse might represent Christ to the world through your marriage. What comes to mind? What might be required of you in order to realize your hopes? What might you gain by prioritizing your shared purpose over individual desires?

Prayer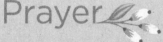

Ask God to:

- help you prioritize your spouse's needs above your own and model sacrificial love in your marriage.

- give you a heart that is quick to forgive your spouse, even in the little things, and for patience to bear with your spouse in love.

- give you insights on how to be a source of redemption in your spouse's life, encouraging them to pursue righteousness and holiness.

- unite you and your spouse and make both of you willing to put aside individual desires so you can focus on your shared purpose to represent Christ to the world.

CHAPTER 8

Humility That Heals

I grew up in a church where everybody knew everybody—which meant we were all up in each other's business. If you had a crush on a boy or were acting up, you could be sure someone would tell your parents about it. If a husband or wife had an affair and the couple was in counseling, word spread fast. But being in each other's business also meant you could count on having a meal train for months if you had a new baby or were dealing with cancer. Plus, chances were good that someone had the spare car part you needed and would gladly give it to you. So while we weren't perfect, we did do our best to love God and live in community with one another.

My mom often tried to get my three sisters and me to tag along with her when volunteering for women's ministry events. One or two of us usually weren't too hard to convince. We'd show up early, set up tables, prepare food, and spend time with the other women in the church. Anette was one of those women who was a regular attender or volunteer at these events. She was an older woman who always came to church alone, even though she was married.

Around the church, we often talked about Anette with sympathy and respect. How on earth was she able to be so strong while being dealt such a short straw? After all, in the women's Sunday school class, she would regularly ask for prayer for Jim, her alcoholic husband, who refused to attend church with her. Although many of us had never seen Jim, I imagined he was a pretty awful person for leaving his wife hanging like that. But then something unthinkable happened—Jim came to church.

I remember trying not to stare but wanting to reconcile the older man who stood across the room from me with the rumors I had heard about him for years. He was quiet and had a cautious look about him, although I could tell he was making an effort to interact with people his wife had known for years. It couldn't be easy walking into a new place, knowing that your reputation had gotten there years before you did. That said, the church was more than excited to greet Jim and welcome him in.

Not long after that first Sunday, Jim started to get help for his drinking by attending addiction support groups and meeting with the pastors of the church for counseling and spiritual guidance. The church, especially the women's Sunday school class, could hardly believe that after all these years, Anette was finally getting what she had dreamed of for so long. What a gracious gift from God!

Or so we thought. Within a year, the unthinkable happened again when Anette decided to leave Jim—and the church.

As it turned out, Jim's recovery changed the dynamic in their marriage, which had some unexpected consequences for Anette. She had become accustomed to her role as a revered churchgoer, which also included being the head of her household and spiritual leader of her family, since Jim's alcoholism prevented him from doing so. And she was used to the sympathy and praise she received on a regular basis for remaining strong in such an unfortunate situation. But now that Jim was taking steps to change his life for the better in overcoming his addiction and growing spiritually, Anette no longer had the same sympathy-based respect she'd once had. Not that anyone's opinion of *her* had changed, but it was understood that her life no longer had the same hardships it once had, and we were happy for her.

What we didn't realize for all those years was that Anette, in an understandable and human way, had a strong sense of superiority over her husband. She was the strong and faithful one who had never fallen into addiction. And many of the people around her saw her that way too. Over time, being the strong and faithful one in a difficult situation became Anette's identity, and she liked being seen as an inspiring spiritual leader. But when, through the grace of God, Jim started to turn his life around, the idea that Anette was superior to Jim began to evaporate. And before she knew it, Anette lost her source of identity. So she left her marriage.

While it may be tempting to shake our heads at what happened to Anette, we may not realize that many of us have something in common with her when it comes to faith. In fact, Anette's inability to see that she and her husband were both equally fallen and in need of grace was an issue so prevalent in Jesus' day that he addressed it in a parable.

The Parable of a Father and Two Sons

Both Christians and non-Christians are quite familiar with the story. We often refer to it as the "parable of the prodigal son" or the "parable of the lost son." But instead of the story being about only one son, I think Jesus is intentionally teaching us a lesson about *two* sons—one who is lost and clearly needs grace and forgiveness, and another who is convinced he doesn't need forgiveness at all.

In the first part of the story, the younger son demands his inheritance early, before his father has even died. He essentially says, "I couldn't care less about you. Just give me my half of your stuff, and then I'm out of here." And instead of driving him out in anger, the father bears this rejection and gives the son what he asks for. Meanwhile, the older brother remains with his father and keeps on doing what any good son would.

When the younger brother exhausts his inheritance and comes to the realization that his sinful autonomy has led only to ruin and pain, he devises a plan to earn his way back into his father's home and hopefully appease him: "I will set out and go back to my father and say to him: "Father, I have sinned against heaven and against you. I am no longer worthy to be called your son; make me like one of your hired servants" (Luke 15:18–19).

But we know how this goes. When the father sees his son approaching from a long way off, he is filled with compassion and runs to embrace his son. The father won't even listen to his son's plan to earn his way back. Instead, the father throws a feast and invites everyone to celebrate his son's return. But not everyone is in a celebrating mood: "The older brother became angry and refused to go in" (Luke 15:28).

The next thing we know, the scene has cut to the older son, who refuses to enter the house and enjoy the feast. When the father finds the older son sitting outside and pleads with him to come in, the older son reveals his resentment and jealousy:

> "Look! All these years I've been slaving for you and never disobeyed your orders. Yet you never gave me even a young goat so I could celebrate with my friends. But when this son of yours who has squandered your property with prostitutes comes home, you kill the fattened calf for him!"
>
> "My son," the father said, "you are always with me, and everything I have is yours. But we had to celebrate and be glad, because this brother of yours was dead and is alive again; he was lost and is found." (Luke 15:29–32).

The older brother is essentially saying to the father, "How dare you use our wealth like that!" Remember, since the younger son had already received his inheritance, everything left of the father's estate would eventually go to the older son. So, feeling protective over his future inheritance—which he believes he's earned—the older brother feels he should have a say over the father's things.

Part of what Jesus is telling us is that both sons wanted the same thing; they just went about getting it in very different ways. They wanted only what the father could give them rather than the father himself. They used the father to get what they truly desired. The younger son tried to secure status, power, and wealth through autonomy and worldly pursuits. When that failed, he hoped to earn his keep by being a servant. The older son wanted the same status, power, and wealth but tried to earn it through loyalty and obedience. In the end, both sons found themselves unhappy with the outcome of their efforts.

On his return, the younger son receives a lavish welcome, but it's not because he agrees to conform through obedience, as his brother has. He is welcomed and celebrated because he finally realizes what he has been missing—the father himself. Jesus is trying to drive the point home that the gospel isn't like any other religion. It isn't about earning our way into God's good graces, with eternal life in heaven as a reward. Nor is it about getting all the material benefits we can get out of our relationship with God while we're on earth. Jesus told this parable to challenge everything his listeners—a mix of tax collectors, sinners, and Jewish religious leaders—believed about who merits God's favor and how it's gained. He wanted them to understand that no one is superior, that we all have equal standing before God, and that we all need grace.

Of course, we know the Bible teaches that living in sin is wrong, but what we often fail to recognize is that it's also possible to spend our whole lives working to obey God (just as the older son tried to obey the father) and completely miss God. The older son did what we often do, which is to put our faith in our own capacity to be good. When we put our faith in our ability to follow the rules—to earn favor—we cut out the need for Jesus and the gospel altogether.

Everyone could clearly see the younger son's sin, and when this son realizes he has been missing out on a relationship with the father all along, he decides to leave his old life behind. It meant completely humbling himself—asking for help and forgiveness when he knew he didn't deserve it.

Jesus tells the story of the two sons to compare their unique misconceptions about their need for the father. He shows us that the way to the life we long for is not through self-indulgence, but it's *also* not through conformity. The two sons both had it wrong. Instead, our true inheritance—what brings us lasting joy—comes through a loving relationship with God the Father. Not only that, but our relationship with the Father is possible through his initiation alone. Notice how it was the father who humbled himself when he took the initiative to seek out both of his sons. The father ran down the road to meet the younger son on his return, and the father went out to talk to the older son when he refused to join the feast.

What may have surprised those listening to Jesus' story at the time was that it was the younger son who ultimately joined the father in his house. Because he chose to humble himself and seek the father's grace, he was welcomed home with open arms. Jesus leaves the story open-ended for the older son who, at the end, is still sitting outside, refusing to go in and celebrate his brother's return due to his own pride and stored up resentment.

Sadly enough, this is exactly what we saw with Anette and Jim. Yes, Jim had lived in sin for many years. No one could deny that, not even himself. But when he humbled himself and sought a relationship with the Father, he was welcomed in and everyone celebrated. What a wonderful thing it is when we realize how desperately we need the Father's grace!

In comparison, Anette had an extremely difficult time understanding and accepting her own need for grace since, like the older brother in the parable, she had faithfully sought to live a good life she could be proud of. Her inability to comprehend her own need for grace not only caused her heart to harden against her husband, but it also hardened her heart toward God.

Even if the details of our story differ from Anette's story, the heart issue she faced is one that many of us face when we fail to acknowledge that we, too, are very much in need of grace and forgiveness. Instead, we put our faith in our own superiority, which not only keeps us separated from the Father but also has the potential to make us act like a bully to our spouse.

Sense of Superiority Assessment

Chances are there are times when both you and your spouse have felt superior to one another—that you know more, are more righteous than, are more mature than, or are a better person than your other half. The important thing is to be aware of these feelings and to notice when they might be turning into a mindset.

Listed below are ten examples of behaviors that characterize those with a superiority mindset. As you read through the list, consider any recent behaviors or tendencies you recognize in yourself.

You may have a sense of superiority if you . . .

- **constantly criticize.** You frequently criticize your spouse's choices, actions, or decisions and believe your way is always the right way.
- **lack empathy.** You dismiss your spouse's feelings or concerns and believe your emotions and needs are more important or valid.

- **dominate decision making.** You tend to make decisions in the relationship without considering your spouse's input or desires, assuming that your judgment is superior.
- **interrupt and disregard.** You frequently interrupt your spouse during conversations or discussions and fail to value their perspective or ideas.
- **are defensive and shift blame.** Whenever conflicts arise, you consistently deflect blame onto your spouse or circumstances and rarely take responsibility for your actions.
- **mock or ridicule.** You belittle your spouse by using sarcasm, mockery, or ridicule when talking to or about them.
- **set unrealistic or one-sided standards.** You expect your spouse to meet unrealistic standards or goals that you wouldn't apply to yourself.
- **ignore your spouse's contributions.** You neglect to acknowledge your spouse's contributions to the relationship, whether these contributions have to do with household chores, childcare, or other responsibilities.
- **compare your spouse to others.** You constantly compare your spouse to others, highlighting their flaws or shortcomings.
- **refuse to compromise.** You're unwilling to compromise and insist on getting your way in most situations.

Healthy relationships are built on mutual respect, equality, and a willingness to work together as partners. If you recognize any of these behaviors in your own life, spend a few minutes in prayer, giving them over to God and asking him to help you change this mindset.

Superiority Is a Bully

My kids get bullied sometimes. As a parent, it's a terrible, gut-punchy feeling to see my kid step off the bus and immediately know something's wrong. They look up at me with red, teary eyes that essentially say, "Where were you when I needed you?"

Then I say, "Hey, kiddo, are you okay? Did something happen?" and the story comes tumbling out. Maybe another kid called them short and weak, took the prize they earned in class, or excluded them from a game at recess.

My initial reaction is to get *all* the details. Who was the bully? What exactly did they say? What did you say? Was there a teacher around? Did you tell the grown-up? Are you okay?

No matter what the bullying was ultimately about, the conversation almost always ends with me saying something like, "Kids who say hurtful things are often trying to feel better about themselves."

As much as I don't want my kids getting picked on, I know that it happens. I also know my kids are likely guilty of saying unkind words themselves, whether it just seemed funny at the time or they were intentionally trying to put someone down to make themselves seem superior in some way. Although we teach our kids not to do these things, creating ways we can feel superior to others runs deep in our nature, and we don't simply outgrow that impulse as we get older.

In fact, it can show up even in marriage—a lot. It may not look like shoving your spouse on the playground or telling them they look funny, but it definitely shows up in other ways.

Have you ever found yourself ruminating over all the little

things your spouse has done to hurt you, meticulously keeping a mental list of each perceived slight? Perhaps you've even brought up these past grievances during an argument, using them as self-righteous ammunition. Or maybe you've spent an entire day busily completing a lengthy to-do list of household chores, only to feel simultaneously superior and resentful when your spouse has managed to complete only a couple of tasks in a haphazard manner. Or perhaps your spouse crossed a line you knew you would *never* cross, and now you nurse that memory and stoke those feelings of superiority over your spouse. If so, you know what it's like to be a bully in your marriage—to think and say hurtful things to feel better about yourself.

Now, I'm not saying we're supposed to ignore hurtful behavior, shove it under the rug in the name of forgiveness, or pretend to be okay with it for the sake of "keeping the peace." No, we need to deal with these issues, and that includes acknowledging and confronting them. However, we also need to guard against using these occasions to bolster our own sense of righteousness or superiority. Yes, we need to talk openly about past hurts, about the areas where our spouse may be dropping the ball or even engaging in blatant sin. And yes, we may need to seek help and counseling for these things. But we can't be bullies, looking down on our spouse to feel better about ourselves.

When you need to address an issue with your spouse, begin by assessing your own motives, especially if the two of you are in different places spiritually. Guard against enjoying being the bigger person, the person who would never have crossed that line, the person who doesn't need to be forgiven. Instead, pray for humility and seek to align your heart with God's heart.

All of us need this realignment regularly. It's easy to climb up onto your pedestal when you see your spouse failing in ways that may be your strengths, but don't forget that you have failures and weaknesses too. Like the behavior of the older son in the parable, even if the list of ways you have disobeyed God appears to be relatively short, your heart condition is no different from that of those whose list of sins may be longer. God sees the true motives behind your obedience and the self-righteousness you feel when you compare yourself with others.

So if you have feelings of resentment toward your spouse, communicate with them about it, but don't be a bully. Approach them with a humble heart and a desire for reconciliation. Seek God's guidance before, during, and after your communication with your spouse. Ask God to bring you both to a place of full reconciliation and forgiveness—not because you want to come out on top, but because a humble, unified, and grace-filled relationship reflects Christ's own love for you, your spouse, and the rest of the world.

Reflection

- In what ways, if any, do you relate to the relational dynamic of Anette and Jim? For example, is one of you consistently the "good" one or the "bad" one in your marriage? If so, how has this dynamic impacted your relationship?

- In Jesus' parable of the father and two sons, both

sons want something from the father but go about getting it in different ways.

- Which of the two sons most closely represents your own spiritual journey and relationship with God? For example, how is your heart like the heart of the younger or older brother?
- In what ways, if any, have you missed God by trying to earn God's favor—for example, through serving God, trying to be better than others, or trying to do all the right things?

• In your marriage, when are you most likely to act like a bully with your spouse—to look down on them to feel better about yourself? When are you most likely to be humble—to approach your spouse with grace and reconciliation?

Prayer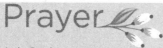

Ask God to:

• help you recognize when you are feeling superior to your spouse so you can make the choice to view them with love, just as God does.

• keep you humble by helping you recognize your own need for his grace and mercy.

- open your eyes to the joys of having a relationship with him rather than focusing only on what you can gain from him.

- provide the courage you need to practice humility and forgiveness in your marriage.

Cultivating Habits of Grace

esus' purpose in taking on human form and coming to earth was to bring us into a reconciled relationship with God. He did that by taking on the fullness of our humanity so he could bear the fullness of our shame. That means he had a complete understanding of what it is to be human, and he empathized with us. Speaking of Jesus as our high priest, the author of Hebrews writes these words:

> For we do not have a high priest who is unable to empathize with our weaknesses, but we have one who has been tempted in every way, just as we are—yet he did not sin. Let us then approach God's throne of grace with confidence, so that we may receive mercy and find grace to help us in our time of need. (Hebrews 4:15–16)

As believers, we are to extend to others this ministry of reconciliation that Jesus modeled for us. We do that in part by making grace the bedrock of all our relationships, and especially in our marriage relationship.

Showering your spouse with grace is essential for your marriage to reflect the relationship the Christ desires to have with his church. When viewed in this way, marriage becomes a ministry of reconciliation in which you have daily opportunities to practice all the graces covered in the previous chapters—forgiveness, vulnerability, unity, and humility. This way, when sparks of frustration and grievance begin to fly, you'll be prepared to extinguish any fires before they set your relationship ablaze.

Journal Exercise: Cultivate Habits of Grace

Take time to identify whatever may be leading you to feel routinely frustrated with your spouse. The issues you identify may be small things, such as your spouse chronically losing their keys, showing up late, or spending too much time with gadgets. Or they may be bigger things, such as a pattern of overspending, using sarcasm or humor to belittle you, or problems related to stress. Use the following questions as a starting point:

- What issues in our marriage are causing anger or frustration to smolder in my heart—for example, behaviors, attitudes, or other patterns?
- Are these things offenses I need to confront, routine annoyances, or something else?

- What makes it hard for me to extend grace to my spouse for these things?

Next, circle two of the issues you identified and use them as your focus for the remainder of the exercise. For each issue, consider any background or underlying factors that can help you understand the reasons for their behavior. For example, if your spouse is regularly overspending, perhaps they were raised in a family in which credit card debt was normal, or the fact that something is a priority to them that's not a priority to you (for example, cozy home furnishings, the best lawn in the neighborhood, nice clothes, and so forth). Write down the name of the first issue you circled, and then underneath it, list three to five background or underlying factors that may be influencing your spouse's behavior. Then do the same for the second issue. For example:

Overspending

- *My husband grew up in a single-parent household with three siblings and often had to go without things he needed.*
- *Wearing new clothes may be a way my husband compensates for being teased about the hand-me-down clothes he had to wear growing up.*
- *My husband is under a lot of pressure at work right now, and buying new things may be a way for him to relax or reward himself.*

Next, consider what a grace-filled response to this issue might be. Note that grace isn't equivalent to remaining silent or turning a blind eye. Instead, it should be a response that demonstrates you understand—or want to understand—where your spouse is coming from; you want to address the behavior in a grace-soaked way; and your goal is personal growth for your spouse and relational reconciliation.

With regard to the issue of overspending, a grace-filled response may be to initiate a conversation about budgeting. Write out what you could say to start the conversation. For example:

> Hey, I noticed you've been spending about $300 a month on nutrition supplements and new workout equipment. I know how important fitness is to you, and I want to support you in that. But I am concerned about how this impacts our budget. Would you be willing to talk about that so we can decide on a realistic budget for fitness gear and supplements?

Whatever the issues are that may be sparking frustration or anger, your goal in addressing them is to fireproof your marriage by showering your spouse in grace. And grace is even more powerful when you make it a habit—something you practice every day.

For the next seven days, make grace a habit by looking for opportunities to shower your spouse with one of the four expressions of grace we covered in the previous chapters—forgiveness, vulnerability, unity, humility. At the beginning or end of each day, use the following prompts to document your experiences:

- I had an opportunity to shower my spouse with grace when . . .
- I offered my spouse grace (forgiveness, vulnerability,

unity, or humility) by . . . Or I failed to offer my spouse grace in the moment, but next time I would do so by . . .

- What I learned about myself and my spouse from this experience is . . .

After completing your seven journal entries, briefly review what you wrote down for each day. Make another journal entry to reflect on the following prompts:

- The most important thing I learned this week about practicing grace with my spouse is . . .
- I want to continue making grace a habit in our marriage by . . .

When we make grace a habit, we give God glory. He rejoices over us as we extend to our spouse and others the same grace Jesus lavishes on us.

Reimagine Your Marriage with Grace

Imagine a future in which grace is your default response and forgiveness, vulnerability, unity, and humility are second nature in your interactions with your spouse. Picture a marriage in which fires of anger and frustration are swiftly extinguished by the waters of grace. This is the promise of grace in marriage—a future in which you and your spouse continually grow closer, becoming a beacon of God's love and reconciliation.

As you work to cultivate habits of grace in your marriage, remember that this is a journey, not a destination. You won't get it right all the time, and that's okay—the very fact that you are making an effort brings glory to God. Just as he rejoices over you when you extend grace to your spouse, your marriage can become a testament to the transformative power of grace.

So keep digging deeper into the graces of forgiveness, vulnerability, unity, and humility. Keep looking for opportunities to extend grace to your spouse every day. And most importantly, keep following the example of Christ. With his help, you can cultivate a marriage that brings glory to God and joy to your hearts.

PART 3

BRANCHING OUT

My friend Jeany had recently returned from her latest mission trip to a country in Southeast Asia, and we were meeting for coffee to catch up. Jeany is an experienced emergency and intervention counselor, and she had gone on the trip to help counsel victims of human trafficking and to lead classes on self-defense and jujitsu. As she told me about her experiences, I thought, *Man, she just can't get any cooler—traveling all over the world, sharing the gospel, helping victims, and teaching martial arts! And here I am, with oatmeal stains on my sweatshirt from the kids' breakfast this morning. And I'm pretty sure there's some on there from yesterday too. I wish I could have the same kind of impact on the world she does.*

After I got home, I switched a load of laundry from the washer to the dryer and started prepping dinner. I had to make a double batch because we were bringing a meal to a neighborhood family who had just come home with their first baby—safe to say, they wouldn't feel like cooking tonight. Josh and David came in through the garage door, followed by David's friend and soccer teammate, Eduardo.

"Is it okay if Eduardo eats here tonight?" Josh asked, his eyes apologizing for the surprise.

"Sure!" I said. "I'm making extra anyway."

After dinner, Josh and I went on an evening walk so we could talk and mentally prepare ourselves for the respite care foster placement we had agreed to host in a couple days. "I took off from work on Friday," I said, "but I do need to be there for one call. Will you and the kids be okay on your own for a little while?"

"Yeah, we'll be fine," Josh said. "Maybe I can take the kids to the splash pad for an hour or so."

"Oh, yeah, good idea. They'd love that," I said.

While brushing my teeth and getting ready for bed that night, I reflected back on the day—on my conversation with Jeany and everything that happened after I got home. That's when I realized that while I've never traveled to Southeast Asia to preach the gospel and teach jujitsu, our marriage did offer me unique opportunities to branch out in faith and show God's love to those around me.

When Josh and I were dating in college, we sometimes stayed up way too late talking about our dreams of going into the mission field together and adopting a bunch of kids. Even at eighteen, we had big plans for how we were going to "bless God" and change the world with our generosity. To be honest, I have to admit that my desire to go into the mission field also gave me a sense of being more spiritually mature than students around me who were studying to be lawyers and businesspeople.

Fast-forward a few years, and God had humbled me and my big plans to help him out. Josh and I were married with two babies, working close-to-minimum-wage jobs, and still living in our same college town. While we served in our local church, it didn't feel like we were anywhere close to living our dream of serving on an overseas mission field. In fact, we weren't even doing that well in our hometown. Our marriage was strained; we were stressed; and I wouldn't have considered myself exceptionally spiritually mature either.

It wasn't until a few more years had passed—when we began to relinquish our idols, hold our dreams with an open hand, and truly find joy in Christ and who he is—that our marriage started to feel healthy. That's when Josh and I began to grow spiritually and started treating each other the way God intended us to as well. We learned how to view ourselves with humility, be vulnerable with one another, forgive faster, and love sacrificially and joyfully. When we truly started to enjoy God, we began to be happier in our marriage as a result. Of course, we weren't, and aren't, perfect, but because of the deeper roots we were growing with Christ as our foundation, our marriage wasn't nearly as rocky as it had been in the past.

After growing and maturing together for a while, we started to feel like our marriage could both be more and do more. We realized we had a unique opportunity for our marriage to reflect Christ's relationship with his church. In fact, we knew we had a responsibility to represent the relationship Christ desired and will one day have with his church. A husband who practices sacrificial leadership and a willingness to die to self represents Christ's sacrifice for us; a wife who serves in humble, intelligent submission exemplifies the way every believer is to follow Christ.

We also had the ability to lean on and support each other in our willingness to serve Christ. If Josh wanted to invite kids from his soccer team to eat homemade pizza at our house while we have conversations with our kids about the character of God or living as a believer at school, then I was 100 percent down to support that. If I wanted to provide a meal for the new mom down the road but was feeling really tired after cooking dinner, Josh could support me by delivering the meal for me.

In the early years of our marriage, we were way more concerned with proving ourselves right in our latest argument than we were about loving and serving those around us. But once Christ became the foundation of our relationship, the love and faithfulness in our marriage only grew. Because of this, we started to focus less on ourselves and more on advancing God's greater kingdom around us.

As you read through the chapters in part 3, I invite you to do two things: (1) look for opportunities to actively support your spouse, and (2) consider together how your marriage might represent Christ to the world around you. Supporting your spouse might start with being attuned to their needs and emotions and stepping in to provide additional support before they even ask, such as putting gas in the car, providing a word of encouragement, letting them know you're praying for them, or simply asking what you can do to help.

Additionally, actions such as being slow to anger, quick to forgive, and edifying your spouse represent Christ both in your home and to the world. When we work to take the focus off ourselves and strive to better love both our spouses and the people around us, we naturally represent Christ through our love, because it's the Holy Spirit in us that enables us to act in self-sacrificial ways. When we represent Christ to others, we do it through the power of Christ and to the benefit of both ourselves and the people he loves.

CHAPTER 9

Growing Roots

Lilly and her husband, Jeremy, were talking and joking as they drove back home from a week at the beach, hearts full after making fun memories together as a young family. As their eighteen-month-old gabbed to himself in the back seat, Lilly decided to start transitioning back to regular life by checking the bills they had coming up.

"Can I have your phone?" she asked Jeremy, explaining that she wanted to log into his banking app so she could check the payments due on their credit cards. Instead of handing over the phone like he usually did, Jeremy started reciting from memory what they owed on each card. "I'd still like to see what our total balance is for the month," she said, holding out her hand for the phone.

"Lilly, I just told you what our balance is," Jeremy responded, which gave Lilly an uneasy feeling. *Why is he being so guarded?* Annoyed, Lilly finally reached out and took the phone from his shirt pocket. Going through their accounts, her heart sank when she saw that most of their savings was gone. Then she also noticed that one of their credit cards had multiple large payments on it she hadn't known about, as if Jeremy had been trying to get the balance back to what it had been, so she'd never notice that the additional charges had been there.

Instantly, she panicked. "Jeremy, what the heck is this? Where's the money that was in our savings account? And what are these monthly payments?"

"I've been helping my dad with payments on a loan for about four months," he finally admitted. Jeremy's father had been almost completely estranged from his family for a couple years at that point, which only added to Lilly's anger and confusion. She sobbed. Then she yelled and said words she later regretted saying in front of their toddler.

Lilly knew this wasn't something they could fix on their own with a few conversations, so she took out her phone and texted Kristen, a Christian friend and mentor who was about fifteen years older and married to their church's youth pastor, Brian. Kristen was someone Lilly knew they could lean on and trust. Lilly asked if she and Jeremy could come over to talk after they got home.

The rest of the drive home was long and quiet. Two days later was their three-year anniversary. Instead of going out to dinner and a movie, Lilly and Jeremy spent it at Brian and Kristen's house. Kristen somehow already suspected that the payments on the credit card weren't to help pay for Jeremy's dad's loan.

"Whose loan is it, really?" Kristen asked.

Jeremy paused for a while before admitting the truth. Turns out, he'd gotten a $15,000 personal loan for some real estate investments he wanted to make. Lilly's sadness quickly turned to anger. Their savings were gone. They were stuck with an almost

$700 monthly loan payment, and their dream of buying a home in the next year or so was gone.

Lilly and Jeremy sat with Brian and Kristen for hours, talking, crying, and praying together. Jeremy was a relatively new believer whose parents' difficult marriage ultimately ended in divorce. They were also prone to unwise spending habits, disjointed communication, and dishonesty with each other. Now Jeremy was repeating those same patterns. At the time he arranged for the loan, he had convinced himself he was making a wise financial decision for his family in the long run. But he realized too late that his dishonesty caused more pain than he ever imagined it would.

Jeremy apologized to Lilly, and they agreed to work together toward mutual financial goals while committing to open and honest communication going forward. Jeremy even asked to be held accountable, giving Brian permission to check in now and then. Of course, the hurt Lilly felt didn't magically disappear after Jeremy's apology. Trust takes time to rebuild. But because of the forgiveness she had experienced through Christ, she forgave her husband, extended grace, and committed herself to fortifying their marriage.

Instead of trying to handle their issues themselves—or worse, letting their anger and resentment fester—Lilly and Jeremy humbled themselves and sought help. They were willing to do the difficult work of admitting they needed help and to seek wisdom from trusted mentors who would prioritize God's truth and their marriage. In doing so, they readied their hearts to be receptive not only to the wisdom of others but also to God's Word. And it was this receptivity—their willingness to allow God's truth to sink deep roots into the soil of their hearts—that enabled them to address their own issues, reconcile, and work toward building a stronger marriage and future together.

Four Heart Conditions

Jesus told a parable about what it looks like not only to have good heart soil, the kind of soil into which God's Word can sink deep roots, but also what it looks like to *not* have it. It's called the parable of the sower:

> "A farmer went out to sow his seed. As he was scattering the seed, some fell along the path, and the birds came and ate it up. Some fell on rocky places, where it did not have much soil. It sprang up quickly, because the soil was shallow. But when the sun came up, the plants were scorched, and they withered because they had no root. Other seed fell among thorns, which grew up and choked the plants. Still other seed fell on good soil, where it produced a crop—a hundred, sixty or thirty times what was sown. Whoever has ears, let them hear." (Matthew 13:3–9)

One of the things that makes this parable unique—not to mention convenient—is that Jesus himself explains its meaning and application. Well, that was easy!

Just kidding. The application, as it relates to marriage, may not be obvious, but I'm getting ahead of myself. First, let's consider how Jesus explains the parable of the sower.

> "Listen then to what the parable of the sower means: When anyone hears the message about the kingdom and does not

understand it, the evil one comes and snatches away what was sown in their heart. This is the seed sown along the path. The seed falling on rocky ground refers to someone who hears the word and at once receives it with joy. But since they have no root, they last only a short time. When trouble or persecution comes because of the word, they quickly fall away. The seed falling among the thorns refers to someone who hears the word, but the worries of this life and the deceitfulness of wealth choke the word, making it unfruitful. But the seed falling on good soil refers to someone who hears the word and understands it. This is the one who produces a crop, yielding a hundred, sixty or thirty times what was sown." (Matthew 13:18–23)

At the time Jesus gave this parable, it was customary for farmers to walk their fields while scattering seed across the entire area, including the borders, to ensure that every inch was covered. Using that technique meant seed would fall on different kinds of soil, some of which was more conducive to growth than others. Jesus uses the metaphor of soil to describe four different reactions people have to the gospel. He wants us to visualize our own receptiveness to his Word and how willing we are to grow and obey after hearing it. Let's take a closer look at the four kinds of soil, and heart conditions, Jesus describes.

Hard Soil

"Some fell along the path, and the birds came and ate it up." (Matthew 13:4)

If you've ever walked a well-traveled dirt path, you know how easily the soil compacts and becomes hard. Jesus equates such hardened soil with a heart hardened against the gospel. A good example of those with hardened hearts in Jesus' day were the religious leaders and teachers who opposed him. Their hardened spiritual condition made it impossible for the good news of the kingdom to penetrate their hearts, which left them vulnerable to Satan.

Those with hardened hearts believe in their own self-sufficiency, have no understanding of their deep need for a Savior, and deny the truth that Christ alone can provide salvation. And with that conviction in their hearts, the devil snatches away the good news, and the hard-hearted never experience new life in the kingdom.

Shallow Soil

"Some fell on rocky places, where it did not have much soil. It sprang up quickly, because the soil was shallow. But when the sun came up, the plants were scorched, and they withered because they had no root." (Matthew 13:5–6)

Seeds that fall on shallow soil look healthy at first but quickly wither because they can't put down roots. Roots enable seedlings to access water and nutrients that not only help them to grow but also keep them from withering in the hot sun. Jesus described those with a shallow heart condition as eagerly embracing the good news at first but quickly falling away when living out their faith becomes difficult or even brings about hardship.

These hearers believe they have experienced the gospel, but they never opened their hearts and allowed the gospel to truly penetrate their lives, which would have led them to obedience and a deeper relationship with Christ, one that could withstand storms and trials. They may show up to worship on Sundays, hear the proclaiming of God's Word, and even have emotional experiences in which they enjoy some of the aspects of God's goodness. But when it comes to allowing God's Word to penetrate and therefore *change* their hearts, they refuse to give over anything to God. In other words, the seeds of God's Word have no root in their lives, so any growth they experience is superficial. When trials arise, their faith quickly withers away, and they move on from Christ to look for a Savior elsewhere.

Thorny Soil

> "Other seed fell among thorns, which grew up and choked the plants." (Matthew 13:7)

Jesus describes those with thorny heart soil as people who hear God's Word but easily lose sight of his goodness and his kingdom. They allow "the worries of this life and the deceitfulness of wealth [to] choke the word, making it unfruitful" (Matthew 13:22). They not only worry about providing for themselves and making their own way in this world, but they are also easily enamored with and distracted by what they can gain through riches. Jesus seems to say that the lure of wealth and prosperity deceives them, and rather than being aligned with God's work, their work is aimed at gaining earthly treasure, which renders their lives unfruitful in God's eyes.

Those with thorny heart soil hear and maybe even believe the Word. The problem is that their hearts are divided. They know what the Bible says, but they don't *love* what the Bible says. Instead, they love earthly things. They know that they *should* find their identity in Christ, but what truly excites them deep down is finding their identity in their status, their possessions, their feelings, and their pleasure.

The conundrum is that they feel guilty about this. How could they not? They know what the Bible says, but the world has a chokehold on them. What they don't realize is that while they're in a chokehold, they're also holding on to the world. Their unwillingness to break free, to abandon the world, prevents them from wholeheartedly receiving new life through Jesus. It's a conundrum C. S. Lewis explored in his classic novel *The Screwtape Letters*.

The novel imagines that Screwtape, a senior demon, is mentoring his nephew Wormwood, a junior demon, in the art of tempting human beings away from God. Screwtape tries to convince Wormwood that it's not necessary to get his human, referred to as the "Patient," to commit big sins; it's simply enough to distract the man for longer and longer periods of time, slowly pulling him away from the "Enemy," who is Christ.

Wormwood's patient knows God's Word, but the idea of living in the world is far more enticing. However, he also knows that the Word condemns the world, so he refrains from fully participating in it. That's the conundrum. At the end of his life, the man reflects and says, "I now see that I spent most of my life in doing *neither* what I ought *nor* what I liked."[1]

There are many times we might find ourselves in the same boat. We may know what God's Word says, but we always feel a *tap tap tap* on our shoulder from the world calling us to join it. So we ask ourselves how much we can participate in to not miss the fun while still doing our best to avoid violating our faith. In

---

1. C. S. Lewis, *The Screwtape Letters* (1942; repr., San Francisco: HarperOne, 1996), 60.

the end, we do neither what we ought nor what we like, and our lives fail to produce fruit.

Good Soil

> "Still other seed fell on good soil, where it produced a crop—a hundred, sixty or thirty times what was sown. Whoever has ears, let them hear." (Matthew 13:8–9)

Finally, Jesus describes the person with good heart soil: "The seed falling on good soil refers to someone who hears the word and understands it" (Matthew 13:23). Jesus is asking us to pause and listen—to hear the Word and allow it to penetrate our hearts and minds. I believe this is the point he's making with the entire parable—that if we listen to the Word and allow it to take root in our hearts, it will grow and produce fruit. Notice that our job isn't to grow the seed but simply to receive it and let it take root. This act of reception requires not only hearing God's Word but also understanding its implications for our lives and allowing it to change us.

In John's Gospel, the apostle refers to Jesus as "the Word": "In the beginning was the Word, and the Word was with God, and the Word was God" (John 1:1). When Jesus speaks of "the word" in the parable, he is speaking of himself, the incarnation of the gospel. Jesus is trying to help us make this connection for ourselves—that by truly hearing the Word, we are receiving him as our one true Savior. And when we understand what we hear, we accept that he is "the way and the truth and the life" (John 14:6). Those who truly hear the Word and allow it to change their lives are those who will grow deep and lasting spiritual roots, and their lives will produce rich and sweet fruit for the kingdom.

The parable makes it clear that Jesus reveals himself to everyone, regardless of the condition of their hearts. No one is left out. But not everyone truly listens and receives the Word with an open heart. Some try to shape and conform it to who they believe God should be for them in order to make him more accommodating to their lifestyle. But those who are truly open to God's Word aren't trying to live in both the kingdom of heaven and our broken world. They truly desire the unfiltered, undistorted Word for all it is, and for none of what it isn't. The receptive hearts—the good soil—hear the Word, truly understand both its benefits and requirements, and embrace a life of discipleship. They don't expect God to make life easy, try to bend their faith to accommodate culture, or prioritize their own desires over God's.

The good soil simply receives. Then the seed does all the work. The seed germinates and puts down deep roots into the soil, giving it a strong foundation so the seedling isn't withered by adversity or choked by weeds. As it grows and matures, it produces good fruit—the visible evidence of its health and vitality. But the soil doesn't produce the seed, much less the fruit, by itself. The soil doesn't really do much of anything at all. It simply remains good soil by being ready to receive the seed. That's what Jesus is asking of us in this parable—that we be ready and willing to receive his Word, to receive him, and to let that gospel seed take root in our lives.

Tilling the Soil for Our Marriage

Jesus used the parable of the sower to help us understand our receptivity to the gospel, but the four soils also provide a compelling metaphor for how receptive we are to the truth of

God's Word in every area of life—and especially in marriage. Whenever we hit a rough patch in our relationship, the condition of our hearts plays an important role in determining how well we'll get through it.

When your spouse drops the ball or straight up wrongs you, you have a choice to make. Will you make your heart ready to receive God's Word by seeking counsel from those who have a gospel-centered focus, who want both justice and grace to abound, and who want your marriage to be a beacon that symbolizes Christ's relationship with the church to the world? Or will you run to those who will tell you only the things you want to hear? "I can't believe she'd do that to you," or "You deserve better than him."

And when it's you who inevitably lets down your spouse, you still have a choice to make about who you'll surround yourself with. Will you choose people who will speak the truth in love and hold up a mirror to the brokenness in your own heart—and will you be receptive to their counsel? Or will you choose those who justify your actions or lead you to question God's Word and his goodness?

Just as we must be receptive to God's Word and allow it to change us in order to grow in our faith and relationship with Christ, we must practice the same receptivity in our relationship with our spouses. To fortify our marriages, we must saturate our heart soil with God's Word and surround ourselves with those who will support our marriages and speak the words we need to hear to help us become more like Christ.

That's the choice my friends Lilly and Jeremy were brave enough to make. Fortunately, their story is one of growth and healing because they chose to humble themselves, seek help from trusted Christian mentors, and open their hearts to God's Word together. Today, their marriage is stronger than ever. They're financially responsible and honest with each other, even when it's difficult. Because they opened their hearts to God's Word and allowed it to take root and transform them, their lives will forever be different.

It is in our willingness to keep our hearts open to God's Word that we become and remain the good soil in Jesus' parable: "Whoever has ears, let them hear" (Matthew 13:9). When we open our hearts to God's Word, we become fertile soil, ready for planting. God's Word penetrates our hearts, and our lives become abundantly fruitful. In John's Gospel, Jesus said these words:

> "I am the vine; you are the branches. If you remain in me and I in you, you will bear much fruit; apart from me you can do nothing. If you do not remain in me, you are like a branch that is thrown away and withers; such branches are picked up, thrown into the fire and burned. If you remain in me and my words remain in you, ask whatever you wish, and it will be done for you. This is to my Father's glory, that you bear much fruit, showing yourselves to be my disciples." (John 15:5–8)

Jesus tells us that unless we keep our hearts open to God's Word, we can never be fruitful—not on our own. And what exactly is fruitfulness? It is simply increasing what was planted. When we allow God's Word to be planted in our hearts, the fruit of the Holy Spirit will overflow and multiply in what we do and say. The apostle Paul writes, "The fruit of the Spirit is love, joy, peace, forbearance, kindness, goodness, faithfulness, gentleness and self-control. Against such things there is no law." (Galatians 5:22–23)

When we allow our thoughts and desires to be shaped by the world around us, our hearts will become hardened, shallow, or thorny, and the good things God wants to multiply in us won't thrive. But when we open our hearts to God's Word and allow it to change us from the inside out, the Holy Spirit will produce love, joy, peace, and so much more in us. The fruit of the Spirit will grow and touch everything around us, including our marriages. This is the way God brings about his glory on earth through us and the way we can best glorify him through marriage.

Reflection

- When Lilly and Jeremy experienced a crisis in their marriage, they knew they needed help to get through it. How have you and your spouse responded when you faced hardships or crises in your relationship? For example, did you seek out help as Lilly and Jeremy did? Try to deal with it on your own? Avoid dealing with it? What happened as a result?

- When you consider the four heart conditions identified in Matthew 13, which of the four do you identify with most in the context of your marriage? In other words, is the soil of your heart hardened, shallow, thorny, or good toward your spouse?

- What intrigues you about reaching out to wise counselors, mentors, or friends for support and guidance in your marriage? What, if anything, concerns you about reaching out? Who comes to mind as someone you could reach out to for support and guidance?

- In what ways have you experienced the fruit of the Spirit (love, joy, peace, forbearance, kindness, goodness, faithfulness, gentleness, and self-control) in your marriage recently? How might you continue to cultivate these qualities?

Prayer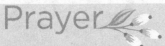

Pray for:

- the humility to recognize areas in your heart where you have been resistant to God's Word.

- guidance and discernment as you seek to align your desires with God's Word and will for your life and marriage.

- wisdom to choose wise, believing counselors, mentors, or friends who will support your marriage and speak the words you need to hear to become more like Christ.

- a heart that is receptive to God's Word.

- the Holy Spirit to overflow and multiply in the things you do and say.

CHAPTER 10

The Significance
of Suffering

As Lacey hung up the phone, she realized she had been pacing back and forth in their bedroom for the entirety of the thirty-five-minute call. She sat down in the chair in the corner of the room and wiped away the tears that were now falling faster and bigger. She knew she was just a few thoughts away from breaking down entirely, but she tried to keep it together, at least for the next few moments, while she considered how to break the news to her husband, Connor.

That's when she heard the garage door open and close and car keys clank on the kitchen counter downstairs. She didn't have time to find the right words. When the sound of quick, happy steps walking upstairs suddenly stopped, she looked up to see Connor standing in the doorway reading her face. He immediately knew.

The birth mom of the baby boy they had hoped to adopt had decided to keep him. Lacey and Connor knew he was her baby, but it felt like they had lost their own child. Today, they wouldn't be leaving for the hospital as they had planned. The bassinet set up in their room would remain empty, and the store tags would remain on the little onesies they had bought. The idea of waking up the next morning to a clean and orderly home, making coffee, and going back to work seemed cruelly normal after having anticipated that their world would be happily turned upside down that afternoon.

Connor and Lacey texted the news to their parents. It wasn't something they wanted to do right then, but they didn't want their parents to worry when the expected photos of the baby didn't come. They cried together and held each other. Lacey laid down to take a nap (she didn't have the will to do anything else), and Connor sat outside until the sun went down.

That evening, they sat together on the couch and ate from a tub of peanut butter pretzels in place of dinner. They didn't have a whole lot to say to each other. They both felt emotionally drained, and talking would only bring back the tears. But after a while, Connor took Lacey's hand and simply said, "Let's pray."

Through Connor's words and in Lacey's heart, they thanked God for the baby who was born that day. They prayed for their almost-son's mom and asked God to bless and support her on this new journey. And they prayed for their own hearts. They asked God to help them have his perspective on their situation and to shift their thoughts away from, *Why is this happening?* and, *But we did everything right.*

The pain of starting over with another adoption was too much to think about. They knew they would have to face that decision soon enough, but tonight they decided to simply allow themselves to cry and to give their pain to God.

Two Kinds of Pain and Suffering

At the beginning of time and the beginning of God's Word, we get a brief glimpse into a time when suffering did not exist. Adam and Eve are walking with God in the Garden of Eden, and everything is as it is intended to be. But only a few verses later, sin enters the world, and consequently, so does pain. God says to Eve, "With painful labor you will give birth to children" (Genesis 3:16). And to Adam he says, "Cursed is the ground because of you; through painful toil you will eat food from it all the days of your life" (verse 17).

The suffering that Adam and Eve experience after the fall is an example of one kind of pain—the kind that is a result of sin. This kind of suffering makes the most sense to us because we understand that our actions have consequences. If we lie on our taxes and then the IRS comes knocking on our door to do an audit, we understand we're suffering because of our own choices.

But there is also another kind of pain—the kind for which there is no identifiable reason or for which the reason may forever remain unknown to us. The Bible acknowledges this kind of pain as well. The Old Testament contains the story of Job, who suffered devastating losses, even though he was "blameless and upright, one who feared God and turned away from evil" (Job 1:1 ESV). And in the New Testament, the apostle Peter writes, "Don't be surprised at the fiery trials you are going through, as if something strange were happening to you" (1 Peter 4:12 NLT). In other words, suffering happens—and sometimes it happens not because of anything we did but because the world is broken.

Chances are you've already experienced both kinds of pain in your marriage many times. You know the pain of consequences from your own actions, as well as the pain that seems to have no reason. Whatever the source of the pain might be, it's important to be aware of the ways suffering can negatively impact your marriage so you can guard against them.

How Suffering Impacts Marriage

While there are an unlimited number of ways that suffering and hardship can negatively impact marriage, three of the most common include communication breakdown, emotional disconnect, and blame.

Communication Breakdown

Stress and anxiety make it difficult to communicate what we're truly feeling, which in turn makes it difficult to connect with our spouses and convey our needs, motivations, and concerns.

For example, when you're laid off from a job, you're finding out in real time how you react to the stress of things such as an uncertain future and financial strain—and your spouse is finding out right along with you. What's running through your mind is, *I'm so scared we won't be able to pay our mortgage next month*, but what comes out of your mouth is, "What were you thinking when you bought brand-name trash bags? Who are we, the Kardashians?" And then an argument ensues. Welcome to communication breakdown.

Communication breakdown in a marriage can manifest itself in many ways. A common symptom many couples experience is a lack of active listening, where partners may hear each other's words but fail to truly seek to understand or empathize with their feelings. Speaking rashly or without consideration can also escalate conflicts, causing emotional harm. Withdrawal or stonewalling, both emotional and physical, is another symptom, as one or both partners might disengage from conversations or the relationship itself. These breakdowns often lead from one misunderstanding to the next, increasing tension and feelings of being unheard or undervalued, all of which can erode the trust and intimacy essential for a healthy marriage.

Emotional Disconnect

Have you ever felt so emotionally exhausted that you lost your ability to care? One time after I had spent most of the day crying, I poured myself a glass of milk at dinnertime, only to immediately knock it over with my elbow. I just stood there and stared at the spilled milk, too emotionally exhausted to do anything about it.

Couples can become that way in marriage too. Prolonged or intense hardships often lead to emotional exhaustion, which can cause us to disconnect both from our own emotions and from other people. When we're consistently overwhelmed by our circumstances, we'll have much less emotional energy to connect with, let alone support, our spouse.

When suffering leaves us emotionally exhausted, it can lead to emotional distance between us and our spouses. Individuals cope in different ways, and sometimes even differently from one hardship to the next. This can leave us feeling like we're at a loss, not knowing how to help or not having the energy to work toward overcoming.

Blame

When we suffer, we often look for a reason in order to find a purpose in it. And when no good reason or purpose can be found, we sometimes cope by identifying someone or something to blame. If only we had more money, more support, or a better spouse, our suffering either wouldn't have happened or wouldn't be nearly as painful.

When husbands and wives identify each other as the reason for their pain (whether it is, in fact, the case or whether they imagine it to be), trust is eroded, emotional wounds fester, and resentment accumulates. All of this poisons a marriage, making it increasingly difficult to find common ground and work together to overcome the hardship.

When we're going through difficulty, it's easy to get angry and even take that anger out on those closest to us, including our spouses. We attach the reason for our pain and anger to something we can understand as a way to cope and make sense of our suffering. For example, during a fight we might say, "I'm lashing out right now because I'm stressed. I'm stressed because we don't have enough money to pay our bills, and we don't have enough money to pay our bills because I can't get the hours I need at work. So if only I had a better job, all our problems would be fewer."

The truth is that even when both you and your spouse are blameless, suffering will still slip through the cracks. The most successful businesspeople can lose everything to unforeseen market conditions. Tightly knit families can lose loved ones to car accidents. And unforeseen circumstances can turn our worlds completely upside down. When suffering strikes, it's tempting to assign blame, but blame almost always makes things worse rather than better in a marriage.

In difficult seasons, every marriage is vulnerable to the negative impact of communication breakdown, emotional disconnect, and blame. However, Scripture gives a broader prospective on our suffering that not only helps us navigate these challenges but also helps us see a greater purpose in what we're going through.

A Purpose Hidden Is Still a Purpose

When suffering comes our way, it's human nature to look for the fastest and most effective way out of it. Perhaps that's why so many Christians love this Old Testament promise: "'For I know the plans I have for you,' declares the LORD, 'plans to prosper you and not to harm you, plans to give you hope and a future'" (Jeremiah 29:11). These words make us feel as though our suffering is temporary and that God's plans for us will soon give us a life filled with good things.

What many of us miss, however, is that God gave this promise at the *beginning* of Israel's seventy-year exile in Babylon. At the time, false prophets were telling God's people, "Hey, don't worry! God says this suffering isn't going to last long. Babylon is going to fall soon, and God is going to bring us right back home!" I'm paraphrasing, of course.

But God intervenes and says (again paraphrasing), "Actually, those prophets are just trying to make you feel better. They're lying to you. Don't listen to them" (Jeremiah 29:8–9). God also says this:

> "Build houses and settle down; plant gardens and eat what they produce. Marry and have sons and daughters; find wives for your sons and give your daughters in marriage, so that they too may have sons and daughters. Increase in number there; do not decrease. Also, seek the peace and prosperity of the

city to which I have carried you into exile. Pray to the LORD
for it, because if it prospers, you too will prosper." (Jeremiah
29:5–7)

In other words, "Settle in and keep living your life. You're going
to be in exile for a while."

Imagine what it would feel like to be taken against your
will to a foreign country where you have nothing and no one.
And instead of immediately rescuing you, God tells you to settle
down and make a life there. Not only that, but he tells you to
pray for and invest in the prosperity in that city. If it were me,
I'd be trying to find the first caravan out of there. But God says,
"No, get comfortable. You're going to be here for a while." And
by "a while" he means seventy years. Depending on your age, it
means you or your loved ones might well be dead by the time
God brings your people home.

That's probably not what the ancient Israelites hoped to hear
in that moment. And I don't know if the idea that there was a
purpose in their suffering would have been much consolation
since the exile itself was a consequence of their idolatry and
disobedience. And yet God still shows them grace. Instead of
abandoning them to their own consequences, God tells them
up front that there is a purpose in it: "'For I know the plans I
have for you,' declares the LORD, 'plans to prosper you and not
to harm you, plans to give you hope and a future'" (Jeremiah
29:11). Even when suffering is a result of sin, God always has a
plan and a purpose.

God's grace and his redemptive plan for us are realities we
can always rely on because we have this promise: "And we know
that in all things God works for the good of those who love him,

who have been called according to his purpose" (Romans 8:28). Whether our suffering is brought about by our sin or as a result of the brokenness of the world, there are at least three ways God uses suffering in our lives—to refine us, to remind us of God's steadfast sufficiency, and to point us to Christ.

Promises through Pain

When the Israelites were exiled to Babylon, their future looked grim. And yet God made them promises that gave them hope.

First, God comforted his people with the promise that he would bring them out of their suffering: "'So do not be afraid, Jacob, my servant; do not be dismayed, Israel,' says the LORD. 'For I will bring you home again from distant lands'" (Jeremiah 30:10 NLT). While the Israelites could expect to live in exile for the foreseeable future, God promised that there would be an end to it. We know that we are living in a broken world, but God promises to make all things new. Our suffering is a result of this brokenness, but it won't last forever.

Second, God promised his people that he heard their cries and that their work in exile was not in vain: "'Restrain your voice from weeping and your eyes from tears, for your work will be rewarded,' declares the LORD'" (Jeremiah 31:16). Never doubt that God hears your prayers and knows what you're going through. He promises to be near, even when what you're suffering is a consequence of your own actions. And he promises to reward the work you do to remain faithful in the midst of your suffering.

Third, God promises that even though the Israelites' suffering was brought on by their sin, he hasn't stopped, and will not stop, loving them: "I have loved you with an everlasting love" (Jeremiah 31:3). During times of hardship, it can sometimes be difficult to feel God's loving presence, but this promise reminds us that he never abandons us, even when our suffering is a result of our own choices.

Finally, in the midst of their suffering, God promises to make a new covenant with his people, which is a reference to the coming of the Messiah and the Holy Spirit. God says, "I will put my law in their minds and write it on their hearts" (Jeremiah 31:33). He promises his people they will one day have a new, more intimate way of knowing him. And this is a promise that is ours today.

Suffering Refines Us

Although suffering was never part of God's original plan for us, he redeems it by using it to refine us. When we suffer, our entire selves are laid bare, including our selfishness, bitterness, hidden motives, dishonesty, and more. Nothing forces us to confront our true selves like suffering does, which is why God invites us to face those parts of ourselves we might otherwise ignore. In the process of self-examination and repentance, God refines our faith and our character.

The apostle Peter acknowledged this redemptive aspect of suffering when writing to early Christians who had been scattered because of persecution:

In all this you greatly rejoice, though now for a little while you may have had to suffer grief in all kinds of trials. These have come so that the proven genuineness of your faith—of greater worth than gold, which perishes even though refined by fire—may result in praise, glory and honor when Jesus Christ is revealed. (1 Peter 1:6–7)

God uses suffering to develop us into better people—people who look more like Jesus and who can love and enjoy him forever.

The apostle Paul put it this way: "We also glory in our sufferings because we know that suffering produces perseverance; perseverance, character; and character, hope" (Romans 5:3–4). Just imagine how our commitment to developing these traits can change a marriage. *Perseverance* might look like a husband or wife who chooses to walk with their spouse through a long season of battling anxiety or depression. *Character* might prompt a spouse to come clean and confess their temptations to look at pornography. *Hope* might help couples look beyond their current pain and anticipate a new and brighter future, whether that future comes in this life or the next. Our hope becomes all the more real in this life when it is placed in Jesus and we allow him to refine us, even as we trust him with what we don't yet know or understand about our suffering.

Suffering Reminds Us of God's Steadfast Sufficiency

Perhaps one of the most difficult aspects of suffering comes when something we love or desire is taken away from us. You love your job but lose it in a round of cost-cutting layoffs. You desire to be healthy yet find yourself battling a chronic illness. You desire a fulfilling and joyful marriage but feel deep pain at every harsh word or unmet need for affection. There is nothing wrong with any of these desires, but we need to remember that our true treasure is found in Christ and in his steadfast sufficiency to cover all our needs.

In marriage, when we face difficult times and our desires are not met—when having children is more difficult than anticipated; when relationships, marital or otherwise, are strained; when financial hardships keep popping up—it's easy to become discontent and lose joy in our relationships. But God wants us to rely on the truths that he is sufficient to cover all our needs and that we can find contentment and joy in him, even in suffering. The apostle Paul affirmed this truth when he was suffering from what he called "a thorn in my flesh": "Three times I pleaded with the Lord to take it away from me. But he said to me, 'My grace is sufficient for you, for my power is made perfect in weakness'" (2 Corinthians 12:7, 8–9).

To rely on God's sufficiency is to choose contentment, even when we don't have what we desire. When we trust in God's provision and focus on his faithfulness rather than focusing on what we don't have, we can find joy in marriage, even during difficult circumstances. This leads us to a deeper appreciation of our spouses, a greater sense of unity in our relationship, and opportunities to reflect our faith in Christ to those who are watching.

Suffering Points Us to Christ

There are pastors who preach that Christ desires for us to live prosperous, happy, easygoing lives. Not only that, but they tell their congregations that Christ will be the source of this prosperity. What's ironic is how they seem to gloss over the fact that the gospel is actually rooted in suffering.

Jesus left heaven and took on human flesh so he could

identify with our suffering and understand our trials and temptations. Not only that, but he also took on the ultimate pain of all our accumulated sins. The apostle Peter writes, "For Christ also suffered once for sins, the righteous for the unrighteous, to bring you to God. He was put to death in the body but made alive in the Spirit" (1 Peter 3:18).

Suffering is deeply embedded in God's central strategy for bringing salvation to the world. The Bible tells us we have a Savior who is familiar with our weaknesses and who shares in our suffering with us (Hebrews 4:15).

As we allow our suffering to reorient us from self-sufficiency to God-sufficiency, God can reshape our marriages into something beautiful that reflects the love of Christ to the rest of the world. Marriage can be a testament to the hope and joy that comes from knowing Christ, and as we walk through suffering together, we can grow in our understanding of what it means to love our spouses sacrificially, just as Christ loved us and gave his life for us.

Navigating Suffering Together

One way God preserves our joy in him in the midst of suffering is by putting us in community with other believers—a community that includes our spouses. When we share our burdens, not only do we help one another, but we also give God glory. The apostle Paul wrote about this in his second letter to the church at Corinth:

> [God] has delivered us from such a deadly peril, and he will deliver us again. On him we have set our hope that he will

continue to deliver us, as you help us by your prayers. Then many will give thanks on our behalf for the gracious favor granted us in answer to the prayers of many. (2 Corinthians 1:10–11)

The Christians in Corinth supported Paul with their prayers, and when God continued to answer those prayers, many people would give God thanks as a result. Paul understood that sharing suffering and bearing one another's burdens give God glory. It is humbling to let people in on our weaknesses, but doing so highlights God's powerful and sustaining grace. When we let others see our struggles, it shows the world how it is God, and not us, who holds us together.

In that same letter, Paul also highlights another benefit of allowing others to share in our suffering—the comfort we receive from God and share with one another:

Praise be to the God and Father of our Lord Jesus Christ, the Father of compassion and the God of all comfort, who comforts us in all our troubles, so that we can comfort those in any trouble with the comfort we ourselves receive from God. For just as we share abundantly in the sufferings of Christ, so also our comfort abounds through Christ. (2 Corinthians 1:3–5)

Paul says that God comforts us in all our afflictions. There is no affliction that God is unaware of or distant from. So we are never alone in our suffering, no matter what the pain or loss might be. But notice the purpose behind God's comfort. As we turn to God for solace and hope, he intends that we will extend that comfort to others who are going through similar trials.

- God comforts us so we can comfort others.
- God shows us mercy so we can be merciful to others.
- God never leaves us alone when we're hurting so we won't leave others when they're hurting.

When we suffer together, we have a unique opportunity to walk through difficult times with our spouse, learn more about each other in the process, and experience more deeply God's sovereignty and provision. Suffering puts tremendous strain on a marriage, but we also have the opportunity to grow closer as we lean on each other in ways easier times don't require.

After the painful news that their adoption had fallen through, Lacey and Conner decided to attend a grief support group at their church. As they shared their sadness, other believers came alongside, comforted them, and prayed for them. They also thanked God that the baby who had nearly become theirs would now be able to grow up with his birth mother, and they continued to pray for their well-being.

Conner and Lacey also chose to volunteer in the children's ministry at their church because, parents or not, they absolutely loved being around children. A little over a year later, God blessed them with the adoption of a baby girl. Once she was theirs, they felt as if she had always been part of their family. And once again, they thanked God for providing for their family.

While we may never fully understand God's purpose in our suffering, we can trust that there *is* a purpose. Suffering can be a refining process, used by God to sanctify us and exalt himself as sufficient. And it's often through our suffering that we can point others to Christ, showing that he is worthy of our trust, knowing that even when our suffering seems to have no purpose,

God is at work. We can also take comfort in knowing that God hears our cries, loves us, and never abandons us. Therefore, we can hold on to hope, secure in the knowledge that God promises to carry us through our suffering and restore us.

Reflection

- Recall a time when you and your spouse went through a difficult season—for example, financial difficulties, the loss of a dream, a relocation to a new city, or health concerns. What were some of the ways you coped with the stress? How did you support each other or fail to support each other?

- Reflect on a time when you suffered because of your own sin or failures. In what ways, if any, did this experience lead to repentance and growth? In what ways, if any, were you tempted to blame your spouse or others for what happened? How did your response impact your marriage?

- Suffering can negatively impact a marriage in at least three ways: communication breakdown, emotional disconnect, and blame. Which of these three do you and your spouse tend to struggle with most when you're in a difficult season? How has it affected your relationship?

- When the Israelites were suffering in exile in Babylon, God gave them an assignment—to keep living their lives and to "seek the peace and prosperity of the city to which I have carried you into exile" (Jeremiah 29:7). Imagine that any current difficulties you and your spouse are experiencing are your "city." What do you think it might mean to keep living your life there and to "seek the peace and prosperity" of that place?

- Overall, how well do you think you and your spouse are doing at navigating hardships and suffering together? To what degree do you let each other and others join you in your suffering? Are you able to both give and receive comfort?

Prayer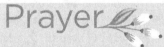

Ask God to:

- help you lean on your spouse during times of hardship and give you the patience and understanding to work through challenges together.

- help you avoid blame and resentment toward your spouse during times of suffering and cultivate a spirit of forgiveness and understanding in you.

- remind you to rely on God's sufficiency and give you patience to wait on his provision.

- give you hope and joy, even in difficult circumstances, and use your suffering to bring glory to him and comfort to others in their struggles.

CHAPTER 11

Overflowing Joy

ight of us were squished like sardines into our Subaru when I got the news. My parents were visiting us for two weeks to meet their newest grandchild, our daughter Cleo. I was about four weeks postpartum but somehow managed to squeeze myself into an old pair of jeans and put on some makeup to feel more like a human being instead of a sleep-deprived milk zombie.

We had decided to spend the day downtown with my sister and her family who were also visiting but traveling in their own car. At some point during the twenty-minute drive, I received an email on my work account. Up to this point, I hadn't been checking work emails because I was still on maternity leave. But when I saw it pop up on my phone and the subject line seemed odd, I decided to open it. While Josh drove the chatter- and laughter-filled car, I silently read the details of my layoff from work, effective immediately.

For about five minutes, I thought it must be a mistake. *They can't possibly be laying me off four weeks into my maternity leave.*

When I finally accepted the fact that I hadn't received the email by mistake, I spent the next few minutes trying to decide how to tell Josh. *Should I tell him in the middle of downtown while we're surrounded by my family? Or should I wait until a quieter moment so we can process the news privately?* But as soon as we piled out of the car and Josh's gaze met mine, there was no hiding it.

"What's the matter, Chels?" he said, looking at me intently.

I thought I could keep my cool, but the breath was shallow in my lungs, and I felt like I had swallowed a golf ball. Before I could even answer, my eyes welled up with tears. "I think I just got laid off," I managed to get out.

"Really?" he said, going through the same initial disbelief I had. Then he pulled me in and hugged me for a long time. "Hey, we'll be okay," he said reassuringly. "God has always provided for us, and we have no reason to believe he won't now."

Not about to pretend that my family wouldn't see my tear-stained face, we caught up to them and told them the news. They hugged us, encouraged us, prayed for us, and reassured us that they would be there to support us in whatever way we needed it.

As the breadwinner for our family, I had a lot on my mind. I mourned the fact that I'd have to start a new job search during what was supposed to have been my maternity leave. I also just really liked my job! But at the same time, I felt what I can only describe as a blanket of peace. I felt wrapped in peace and reassurance, like the swaddling we were doing with Cleo to keep her from startling, like so many newborns do. I knew that God was good, and no matter what our financial situation turned out to be in the near or distant future, he would be at work for our good.

The Slippery Nature of Happiness

Have you ever had a dream in which you want to run to something that is nearby but you just can't get your legs to work? It's like your feet are stuck in peanut butter, and no matter how hard you try, you never manage to get closer to it. That's what our pursuit of happiness is often like. We have a vision of what we believe will make us truly happy—a bigger paycheck, a child, a more fulfilling relationship—but the more we pursue happiness, the more it seems to evade us. Or we *do* get what we were chasing, only to discover that it doesn't give us the feeling of happiness we were hoping for—like picking up a glass of Sprite at dinner only to take a sip and realize it's just plain water. What we thought we were getting turns into disappointment.

Unhappiness doesn't seem to have the same fleeting nature though. In fact, it can be quite sticky. Unhappiness is what we experience when life fails to live up to our expectations—and we begin to doubt it ever will. We can be patient for a little while as we work toward our goals, but when we start to realize that our goals are increasingly out of reach or simply not as satisfying as we thought they'd be, unhappiness can feel like a permanent resident rather than a temporary guest. And that's when our emotional health and well-being can begin to slip—because happiness is slippery by nature.

I've experienced many moments of both happiness and unhappiness in my life—times when all I wished for was to get married, the happiness of being united to the one I love, and then the times when I was married and found myself still being weighed down by unhappiness. Times when my dream of a higher-paying job came true, only to find myself stressed and unable to fall asleep at night because of the increased pressure and responsibilities of a higher-paying job. Times I dreamed of a house full of children, only to be scrolling social media while holding my baby and feeling jealous of the vacation photos posted by someone I've never met.

Yes, happiness is slippery, but God offers us something so much better than happiness—the lasting joy that comes from our security in Christ.

The Joy of Our Security in Christ

I was sitting in my college chapel one morning before the sun had even come up. I was wrestling with the idea of knowing without a doubt whether my salvation was secure. Up until then, I had a works-based approach to faith: If I felt that I had obeyed God's Word well enough and for long enough, then I was in a "good place" with God. If, however, I felt that I hadn't been especially self-sacrificing or had slipped up and sinned, then a cloud of doubt hovered over me, and with it came the fear that my salvation had never truly existed.

However, as I prayed and read my Bible in that chapel, it felt almost as though God had bent down and whispered in my ear, "Relax. Just enjoy me. If you simply enjoy me, everything else will fall into place."

I meditated on that for a while, and it made a lot of sense. God is the creator. He is true, he is pure, lovely, admirable, and praiseworthy. There is so much goodness about him—how can he not be a source of joy? And if I truly found my joy in him, then my desire for lesser things would naturally fall into place, because those things would be less desirable when compared with God's beautiful nature and all he had to offer me, such as freedom, peace, love, restoration. The things I was chasing for happiness can't hold a candle to him.

Of course, that doesn't mean other things didn't make me happy. Late-night milkshakes with friends, getting engaged to Josh, and adopting our first puppy all made me extremely happy! But when compared to the joy of knowing God, I could see them for what they truly were—fragments of happiness. For example, imagine putting a box with holes in it over a really bright light. Each ray of light streaming through the holes would be just a fragment of the greater light within, and it would be dull in comparison to that light. The joy we have in knowing God is like that really bright light, and the things that make us happy on earth are like the smaller rays of light. Although they pale in comparison to God himself, they are still good gifts. And they become even more meaningful when we know these good gifts stem from God's goodness itself.

God's invitation to enjoy him—to make him my highest joy—also helped me realize that if I couldn't earn my salvation (Ephesians 2:8–9), then I couldn't lose it either. I could finally rest in the knowledge that God was not only everything I needed, but he far surpassed anything I could ever want. And since there was nothing I could do to change my standing with Christ, how much less could my own doubts or unhappy circumstances do so? With my standing in Christ secure (because there was nothing I could do to change it), and my happiness anchored in him (because he forever radiates the characteristics that truly make my heart happy), the slippery nature of my happiness began to shift into the resilient nature of joy.

In our search for happiness, we often overlook the profound

power of joy. In his second letter to the church at Corinth, the apostle Paul eloquently captures the essence of Christian joy, even when facing challenges and suffering:

> We have this treasure in jars of clay to show that this all-surpassing power is from God and not from us. We are hard pressed on every side, but not crushed; perplexed, but not in despair; persecuted, but not abandoned; struck down, but not destroyed. We always carry around in our body the death of Jesus, so that the life of Jesus may also be revealed in our body. (2 Corinthians 4:7–10)

Paul's imagery conveys this resilient nature of joy, which I imagine as something like a life vest that buoys us up when we're tossed around in the stormy seas of life. While joy can't shield us from suffering, it can empower us to rise above it, knowing we are unsinkable through our unwavering faith in God.

The Paradox of Joy in Sadness

Andrea came inside and put the box of her grandmother's things on the kitchen counter. She'd sort through everything and put it away later. She didn't have the emotional energy to think again about everything that had just happened that month. For now, she needed to sit on the couch and maybe have a pint of ice cream.

Growing up, Andrea and her grandma were very close. She'd spend many weekends at her house. On Sunday mornings, her grandma would pick her up for church and then bring her back to her house for the afternoon. Andrea knew her grandmother's house like the back of her hand and even had her own room there, where she'd sleep when she stayed for a few weeks every summer. Once Andrea was grown and lived farther away, she made it a point to call her grandma every week and catch up. She loved just listening to her grandma's stories about the neighbors she visited or her cat's bad behavior. Talking with her grandmother reminded Andrea of simpler times and helped her relax after a long and stressful week at work.

Andrea's husband, Rob, walked into the room a few minutes later. "Do you want me to help you put Grandma's stuff away?" he asked.

"I guess I shouldn't put off the inevitable," Andrea sighed as she pulled herself off the couch.

She grabbed the box, brought it into their room, and spread out the eclectic collection of jewelry, photos, and trinkets on the bed. She picked up a photo of her and her grandmother and turned it over. "Andrea, 6 years," was scribbled on the back in her grandmother's handwriting. Tears started to well up in her eyes again just as Rob walked into the room. "Well, that didn't take long," she said, smiling at Rob through her tears. He smiled back sympathetically.

"I just can't believe she's not here anymore," Andrea said. "I should have gone to see her more."

"She knew how much you loved her," Rob said. "She knew you would have visited her more often if it hadn't been for the distance. And she *loved* your phone calls! I know they meant a lot to her. I *promise* that she knew how much you loved her." He paused and took a moment to add what he knew Andrea needed to hear, "And she loved you too. She's with Jesus now, and she's never been happier."

Andrea gathered herself and took a deep breath. "You're right. I do like picturing her being happy and whole in heaven. She always talked about what it would be like to meet Jesus someday. I'm glad she doesn't have to wait anymore. And I know someday we'll see her again."

Mixed in with Andrea's sadness and grief was a thread of joy. As much as she loved and missed her grandmother, she knew her grandmother was at home with Christ and that they would be reunited one day. Her experience is one that demonstrates how sadness and joy aren't mutually exclusive. We can choose to hold on to joy even as we grieve painful losses and navigate difficult seasons.

And yet some of us tend to feel guilty when we're struggling—as though we need to "put on a good face" during times of sadness to show that we trust in God's sovereignty. But the Bible makes it clear that it's possible to experience joy right smack-dab in the middle of experiencing sorrow.

Perhaps the best examples of this are found in the psalms. David's prayer for deliverance in Psalm 57 expresses a range of fear, pain, and sadness. But David also beautifully intertwines praises to God with his sorrows:

> I am in the midst of lions;
>> I am forced to dwell among ravenous beasts—
> men whose teeth are spears and arrows,
>> whose tongues are sharp swords.
>
> Be exalted, O God, above the heavens;
>> let your glory be over all the earth.
>> (Psalm 57:4–5)

It's almost as though David is saying to God, "I feel as if my life couldn't get any worse, but that doesn't change the fact that you are good. Even though I don't know why this is happening to me, I will find rest in you because I know you have all the answers."

It is not putting on a brave face when we're struggling that demonstrates our faith in God's sovereignty; it's choosing to allow both our sorrows and God's goodness to coexist. That's the paradoxical nature of joy—we can experience it even in the midst of sadness and hardship. And this faith is what differentiates us from those who don't follow Christ—we can tap into the abundant resources available to us through Jesus. Every experience of suffering is also an invitation to delve deeper into the riches of joy that await us. Even when experiencing sorrows, we can seek comfort from our Creator and rest in the hope that he can and will make all things new.

Anchored to an Unshakable Future

As Christians, we have the opportunity to be joy specialists because we have access to our Creator, who is the source of all joy. We can savor a delicious meal, appreciate physical comforts, and gaze at the beauty of the world, all while recognizing that they are mere glimpses of the joy to come when we are reunited with Christ. We can choose joy even in difficult circumstances because we know that joy isn't limited to slippery moments of happiness but is rooted in the sure hope of our future. This anticipation of our unshakable future fuels our joy and sets us apart as bearers of God's light and love in a world longing for lasting joy.

When I lost my job, I could have—trust me—easily spiraled into a panic, frantically trying to piece together our income, the way our lives functioned, and even my identity as the bread-winner. In those moments, I wasn't just losing my job; I was at risk of losing my sense of security and identity. But through the grace of God, I was gently reminded that it is he, not an employer, who holds my world together. The apostle Paul writes, "[God] is before all things, and in him all things hold together" (Colossians 1:17). Because my security is anchored in Christ and I am never in danger of losing him, my heart didn't sink into per-manent despair with the unexpected loss. Yes, I allowed myself to mourn the loss, but I also chose joy by focusing on my hope in an unshakable future with Christ.

Joy in Action

When Katie's alarm went off at 5:30 a.m., she quickly turned it off before it woke her husband sleeping to her left and the baby sleeping in the bassinet to her right. She tiptoed out of the room, slowly closed the door behind her, and grabbed her yoga mat. Twenty minutes later, she rolled up her mat and took a quick shower. By now, Dan was up scrambling eggs and brewing cof-fee. Katie grabbed a cup and sat down to read her Bible for a few minutes before the baby woke up. Within the next hour, she had finished her morning devotion, changed and fed the baby, helped get their two other kids ready for school, made Dan's lunch, and kissed everyone but the baby goodbye as Dan left to drop off the two older kids at school before heading to work.

After waving goodbye, Katie turned around and saw the debris left in the aftermath of their busy morning routine. She sighed and went to work picking up pajamas, putting breakfast plates in the dishwasher, and attaching crumpled-up drawings from the kids' backpacks to the fridge. She started a load of laundry, and after the house looked somewhat reasonable again, she decided to take the baby on a short walk to get some fresh air. When they got back, Katie put the fussy baby down for a nap and then sat on the couch for a moment to catch her breath. Just then her phone buzzed. It was a text from Dan: "Thank you for everything you do for us, Katie. You are truly the most amazing wife and mom. I know changing diapers and making lunches may not always feel like the most rewarding work, but you make us all feel so loved and cared for. And you somehow manage to do it all with joy. I called a sitter on my way to work so we can go out to dinner and have a date night tonight. Can't wait! Love you."

Katie lingered over the text for a while, feeling thankful for her husband's kind words and wondering where they should eat that night. Dan was right—most of her days were draining, and no one gives out awards for the best diaper change or most nutritious school lunch. But she knew that graciously serving her family in this phase of life was where she was needed, and she found joy in the idea of loving them well. She didn't always realize it, but her family felt her underlying joy, and it set the tone for many of the interactions in their family. Her joy, rooted in Christ, radiated beyond herself and touched everyone close to her.

Our access to God's unlimited joy is also access to God's unlimited strength. The prophet Nehemiah acknowledged this when he wrote, "The joy of the LORD is your strength" (Nehemiah 8:10). Choosing joy is what gives us the strength we need to take on life's challenges, both big and small. We can self-sacrificially serve our family, even when moments of recognition are few and far between. We can face an unknown future, knowing that God is good and our ultimate future with him is secure. And we can hang on to joy in loss and sadness, knowing that while the things of this world are temporary and fleeting, our relationship with Christ is eternal.

Every day, we can make the choice to bring this joy into our marriages and allow it to shape the way we share our burdens, interact with each other, and sacrificially serve each other. And the purpose of this overflowing joy doesn't end with marriage. It's meant to be shared and multiplied, to become a beacon of hope to those around us and a testament to the transformative power of Christ's love. When our joy becomes contagious, we'll draw others closer to the source of our true and lasting joy.

Through our acts of service and willingness to share the gospel, Christian couples become living testimonies of God's faithfulness and provision. We can shine as lights in a world that feels overwhelmed by darkness and despair. Our unwavering joy is what sets us apart, attracting others to the hope that can only be found in Christ. Our joy is a gift to be shared, an overflowing stream that nourishes and uplifts everyone it touches.

God never intended for us to escape from the world and its troubles after we experience salvation in Christ. The promise of Scripture is that God loved the world so much that he gave his one and only Son to save it (John 3:16). That's why we're still here—to be ambassadors of God's redemption, reconciliation, and joy to the world.

Reflection

- What are some of the things you are pursuing to find happiness? What comes to mind when you think about shifting your focus from pursuing happiness to cultivating joy through your relationship with God? What might such a shift in focus require of you?

- Reflect on a time when you experienced joy in a difficult circumstance. What were some of the factors that contributed to your ability to find joy in that situation?

- How might embracing the concept of joy as a resilient and unshakable force impact the way you handle challenges and uncertainties?

- Who comes to mind when you think of joy as a source of strength? How does that person embody joy? Use joy to serve others? Use joy to persevere in hardship?

- In what ways would you enjoy putting joy into action—embodying Christ's love by serving your family or extending a helping hand to someone in need?

Prayer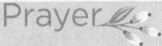

Ask God to:

- help you find your joy in him, even when circumstances in your marriage or daily life are difficult.

- guide you in pursuing true and lasting joy rather than chasing after fleeting happiness.

- empower you to anchor your security in him, knowing that he is the one who holds everything together.

CHAPTER 12

Living with Open Hands

t was a warm evening in late May, and Josh and I had just said good night to the last of our friends who were heading home after small group Bible study at our house. We were getting David and Evy ready for bed—coaching them to brush their teeth longer and get their pajamas on, and saying, "Okay, really, it's time to start calming down," once they finally got upstairs to their bedrooms. As I kissed the kids good night, my phone buzzed with a text from our social worker, Jennifer.

She described two little boys who were currently in the hospital and needed a foster home, indefinitely, starting that night. My heart raced, but I tried to sound calm and collected on the phone. I asked for what little additional information she could give me, such as their ages, why they were coming into foster care, any disabilities or health issues, and so forth. Even though she couldn't tell me much, Josh and I had to make a snap decision: Do we say no to this placement, watch some Netflix, and get a good night's sleep, just as we had planned to spend the rest of our evening? Or do we say yes, knowing very little about the boys who needed a home indefinitely?

I told Jennifer that Josh and I would talk, and I'd text her our answer in a few minutes. We talked and prayed, and then we said yes—although I half expected Jennifer to have already found another willing family in the few minutes we had taken to discuss it, which had happened many other times. But that wasn't the case tonight. Jennifer texted back a few minutes later to tell me the boys would be at our house by midnight.

Slightly shocked, Josh and I gaped at each other with wide eyes that communicated, *Wow, okay. This is really happening.*

After the boys arrived and we got them put to bed, I couldn't help but cry. I was overwhelmed with thoughts about how scary this must be for them, wondering if we had made a mistake and what our lives would be like in the days to come.

I won't lie, the next few months weren't easy. Overnight, we doubled the number of children we cared for, which would have been challenging under the best of circumstances. While we had completed many hours of training to become licensed foster parents, we were now learning in real time what it was truly like to parent children who had suffered trauma. Shortly into their placement, we were also told that one of the boys had previously been diagnosed with oppositional defiant disorder (ODD) and autism. At the time, the news came as a relief because a formal diagnosis meant we were able to get specific help right away.

Every day, Josh and I woke up and gave 110 percent until all four little heads hit the pillows each night. As demanding as that time was, Josh and I knew we were exactly where we were supposed to be. We knew we were expending our energy out of obedience, and that was comforting in and of itself.

As it turned out, the boys were with us only from the end of May through August, but we felt incredibly blessed to have them in our lives for those few months. Our small group and church supported us and loved us through the transition, for which we were very grateful. Additionally, our biological children, David and Evelyn, were exposed to a whole new level of need that they might otherwise have never experienced, especially at such a young age. While they lived through many moments that weren't easy for them, we all had a great opportunity to practice obedient generosity as a family and open our home in faith while loving the boys during an extremely difficult time in their lives.

Called to Generosity

When I was a kid in church, I thought of generosity as something rich people were able to do because they had a lot of excess wealth to give. And because I never imagined myself being rich, I considered generosity to be a wonderful Christian principle that was mainly for others who were more fortunate with their finances. Instead, I could practice Christian virtues such as mercy or exhortation. But my preconceived notion of generosity got turned upside down when I read passages in the Bible such as this one from the apostle Paul:

> Remember this: Whoever sows sparingly will also reap sparingly, and whoever sows generously will also reap generously. *Each of you* should give what you have decided in your heart to give, not reluctantly or under compulsion, for God loves a cheerful giver. (2 Corinthians 9:6–7, emphasis added)

When I read "each of you," it was kind of hard to ignore the fact that Paul was, well, speaking to all of us, including me—no exceptions. And yet it was also somewhat confusing. If God knows that some people have far more wealth or possessions than others, why are we all called to be generous? Not only that, but if God is in control of the world and can choose to bless whomever he wants to bless anyway, why are we still called to be generous and share our own resources with others?

What I eventually learned is that God calls us to be generous because he himself is generous, and he uses our generosity to teach us, change us, and advance his kingdom on earth. Specifically, generosity acknowledges that everything we have belongs to God; generosity is a tool to reach others; and generosity is worship in action.

Generosity Acknowledges That Everything We Have Belongs to God

Generosity can only happen when we realize we have something to give. And we have something to give because God is the source of everything we have. King David acknowledged this truth when he wrote, "The earth is the Lord's and everything in it, the world and all who live in it" (Psalm 24:1). Even if we work hard for a paycheck, the ability to work itself is a blessing from God. God calls us as believers to be generous because everything we have comes from God and belongs to God. Our role is simply to be good stewards of the resources with which he has blessed us.

No matter how much or how little we have, we can be generous by constantly looking for ways to bless others with our resources. This is one of the ways we act on our faith. As James puts it, "What good is it, my brothers and sisters, if someone claims to have faith but has no deeds?" (James 2:14). Generosity might be anything from sharing a meal, babysitting a single parent's kids for free, giving someone a ride, or paying someone's medical bill. Sharing what we have with others is an acknowledgment that everything we have is, indeed, a gift from God.

Generosity Is a Tool to Reach Others with the Gospel

God uses his church to meet the needs of others. When we are generous, we make our faith complete by living it out in concrete ways. We trust that our needs will be met, and we therefore have more than enough capacity to meet the needs of others. By being generous, we're saying, "God, I trust you to provide for me, and so I want to be generous with the resources you've given me. Use me to bring glory to you."

By living out our faith through generosity, we also develop the discipline of holding our blessings with an open hand. This isn't just a onetime action, but it is also a heart posture—an immediate willingness to give. This is how we allow Christ to use our generosity for supernatural change in the lives of others, even when we feel like we don't have much to give. All that's required of us is to be obedient and have faith that God will do the rest. If he can give us eternal life, he can certainly multiply our little into much. We see one of the most powerful examples of this when Jesus and the disciples were surrounded by thousands of hungry people and a small boy offered Jesus his lunch:

> Another of his disciples, Andrew, Simon Peter's brother, spoke up, "Here is a boy with five small barley loaves and two small fish, but how far will they go among so many?"
> Jesus said, "Have the people sit down." There was plenty

of grass in that place, and they sat down (about five thousand men were there). Jesus then took the loaves, gave thanks, and distributed to those who were seated as much as they wanted. He did the same with the fish.

When they had all had enough to eat, he said to his disciples, "Gather the pieces that are left over. Let nothing be wasted." So they gathered them and filled twelve baskets with the pieces of the five barley loaves left over by those who had eaten. (John 6:8–13)

Never think that what you have to offer is too small. When you give to those in need, God can use what you give to change the trajectory of their lives. Your generosity can be a source of hope and encouragement to those who are struggling, and it can help create a better future, not only for those to whom you give, but also for your community and even the world.

Jesus is the ultimate example of generosity. He gave his life for us, and he calls us to follow his example by giving of ourselves and our resources to others. When we're generous, we embody the love and compassion of Christ and share his message of lavish grace with the world.

Generosity Is Worship in Action

What we do with our finances says a lot about what and who we care about, and also what we believe about God. When we hold our finances, our time, and our resources with a tight fist, we're essentially saying, "I don't have enough to sustain my own life and I don't have faith that God will provide for me, so I can't share what I have." But when we choose instead to give generously, we're saying, "God, I'm not sure where more of what I need is going to come from, but I know your character. You are good, all-knowing, and loving. I trust that you will take care of me when I give this away." That is worship in action. It's putting our money where our mouths are and showing that we believe that God is who he says he is—the one who is worthy of our trust, is able to provide for and sustain us, and has plans for us that are far better than our own.

Generosity also holds profound significance for married couples as a unique form of worship we can practice together. When we embrace generosity as an integral part of our relationship, it not only strengthens our bond but also deepens our faith. Through joint acts of giving, we embark on a shared journey, pursuing a common goal and fostering a sense of unity within our marriages. What's more, practicing generosity offers countless opportunities for us to nurture our trust in God's provision and rely on his guidance as we submit ourselves to Christ in giving.

Couples Can Be More Generous Together

For a marriage to thrive, both husband and wife must commit to sacrificial acts of love, consistently seeking to serve one another. Generosity in marriage also requires being lavish with forgiveness, extending grace, and offering second chances. It requires choosing to see the best in our partner, even in their moments of imperfection. It involves fostering an atmosphere of mutual support in which both individuals can freely express their needs, dreams, and fears without fear of judgment or rejection. When we practice generosity in these ways, we grow in spiritual maturity and more fully embody Christ's relationship with the church.

As we mature in our relationships with each other and with Christ, we're also entrusted with the responsibility to represent Christ to the world, pouring out the overflow of our love to others. That's how the love and grace we experience in marriage become channels through which God pours out his love to those around us. Our commitment to serving and caring for others becomes an integral part of our ministry as Christian husbands and wives. We understand that our purpose extends beyond our personal happiness and encompasses the mission of sharing Christ's love through our interactions with others.

Generosity Challenge

The goal of this exercise is to help you strengthen your commitment to generosity and foster a sense of shared purpose by identifying a way to give and serve together.

1. **Identify a generosity focus.** Choose an area in which you'd like to be more generous as a couple. For example, this might involve supporting a local or national charity financially, volunteering at your church, or coming alongside an individual or family in need with financial assistance or other support. Because this is a challenge, whatever you choose should require you to step out of your comfort zone, try something new, or do more than you've done before.

2. **Set a time frame.** Determine the time frame for your generosity challenge. It could be a week, a month, or any duration that works for you.

3. **Create a giving plan.** Discuss how you'd like to give or serve in your chosen area of focus. Consider whether you'll donate money, time, skills, or resources—or a combination of actions. Develop a plan that details your goals and the specific steps needed to achieve them.

4. **Execute the plan together.** Act on your generosity plan as a team. Dedicate the necessary time, effort, and resources to complete your challenge.

5. **Reflect and discuss.** After executing your plan, sit down together to reflect on your experiences. Discuss how the act of giving and serving impacted your marriage, your faith, and your sense of purpose as a Christian couple.

   - How did it feel to give and serve together as a couple in this challenge?

   - In what ways, if any, did the challenge strengthen your sense of unity and purpose?

   - What were the most meaningful moments or experiences during the generosity challenge?

   - How was your faith reflected in your actions during the challenge?

   - How would you like to incorporate ongoing acts of generosity and service into your marriage and daily life?

   - What other areas or causes would you like to explore in future generosity challenges?

6. **Pray together.** Offer a prayer of gratitude for the opportunity to give and serve and ask God for guidance on how to continue embodying faithful generosity in your lives.

Reflection

- Reflect on a time when you were the recipient of someone else's generosity. What did they do for you, and how did it impact you in the short and long run?

- In what ways are you currently practicing generosity in your personal life and marriage? How has God used your generosity to teach you, change you, or advance his kingdom on earth?

- What fears or anxieties, if any, do you have about being more generous with your resources?

- It's easy to imagine how we might be more generous if we had a lot of money or won the lottery, but God asks us to be generous with the little we do have rather than the much we don't have. What are some of the "littles" you do have? How might you and your spouse be more intentional in sharing with others whatever those things are?

Prayer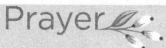

Ask God to:

- open your eyes to ways you can be more generous, whether it be in your marriage, your church, or your community.

- empower you to represent Christ to the world by sharing what you have with those around you.

- show you how you can serve and care for others and make generosity an integral part of your ministry as a Christian couple.

Cultivating Deep Roots and Wide Branches

Growing in spiritual maturity is a great place to be. It means finally shedding many of the old habits that used to weigh you down—things like having to get the last word in arguments or constantly seeking the approval of others. As a wonderful indirect blessing, growing deeper in our relationship with Christ allows us to let go of many of our preconceived notions and expectations of what we hoped our spouses would be for us, and, in turn, we begin to see them through God's eyes instead. Yes, they need forgiveness and always have room to grow when it comes to learning to be more Christlike, but when we see them as someone who has been redeemed by the very person who also granted us forgiveness and a way to know God personally, it really starts to shift our perspective.

Once we start looking to Christ more diligently as our source of joy, we start to release the grip we once had on our spouses, or whatever else we had in mind, when we were desperately hoping for them to be the ultimate source of our security and happiness.

When that mindset begins to shift, we can start enjoying our spouses in the way God intended us to—as a gift that reflects his love for us. That is the type of love that fills our souls and can be deeply satisfying. It's secure, steadfast, and unyielding. And it's in this love that we can feel secure and rooted enough to begin to branch out in faith.

Journal Exercise: Cultivate Love in Action

Take some time to reflect on what your spouse does to make you feel rooted, secure, and supported in your relationship. Use the following prompts:

- I feel *rooted* in our relationship when . . .
- I feel *secure* in our relationship when . . .
- I feel *supported* in our relationship when . . .

For example:

- *I feel rooted in our relationship when my husband and I feel like a team because we can lean on each other when we go through tough times.*
- *I feel secure in our relationship when I tell my wife I made a mistake and she doesn't react in anger but rather forgives me and works with me to make it right again.*
- *I feel supported in our relationship when my husband tells me he's grateful for me and asks how he can help me.*

Knowing that you and your spouse are growing deeper roots in your relationship with each other and with Christ, consider how you might begin to branch out, using your marriage as an extension of your faith. Use the following prompts as a starting point:

- We could invite . . .
- We could volunteer . . .
- We could give . . .
- We could . . .

For example:

- *We could invite different neighbors over for dinner once a week to build relationships in our community.*
- *We could volunteer twice a month at our local food pantry.*
- *We could give more and involve our kids by collecting our pocket change, rounding up small amounts from purchases, and donating the total once or twice a year to the benevolent fund at our church.*
- *We could increase the percentage of our income that we give to the church and to charities.*

For the next seven days, continue looking for ways to both deepen the roots of your relationship with your spouse and branch out by using your marriage as an extension of your faith. At the beginning or end of each day, use the following prompts to document your experiences:

- I helped my spouse to feel rooted, secure, or supported in our relationship by . . .

- My spouse helped me to feel rooted, secure, or supported in our relationship by . . .
- I/we were able to branch out and help others by . . .

After completing your seven journal entries, briefly review what you wrote down for each day. Make another journal entry to reflect on the following prompts:

- The best way I can help my spouse feel rooted, secure, or supported in our relationship is . . .
- The best way my spouse can help me feel rooted, secure, or supported in our relationship is . . .
- The most important thing I learned this week from branching out and helping others is . . .

Branch Out with Grace

As you consider ways God may be leading you to branch out and serve others, keep in mind that you and your spouse may or may not be on the same page about how and when to do so—at least initially. Be careful not to force things or become resentful if the two of you have different ideas or concerns. Instead, follow the lead of my friend Sandra by giving your spouse grace and waiting on God's timing.

Sandra and her husband, George, were missionaries for many years, but she told me that when she first told George of her dream that they would be missionaries, he told her no—that it wasn't for them. He promised her they would support missionaries, but they would never be long-term missionaries themselves. Sandra was devastated because she truly felt that being a missionary was something God had called her to do. But instead of allowing the rift to attack her marriage, she prayed that God would change George's heart.

A couple years later, George did have a change of heart. God called George and Sandra to live in Spanish-speaking countries and help build up local churches. And that's what they did. They learned Spanish and spent many years on the mission field together.

While Sandra was eager to live out her dream of being a missionary, she first had to surrender that dream to God and commit herself to finding peace and joy in Christ, no matter where she was. She also decided to do whatever she could to branch out in faith in their local community in ways George supported.

If you are the first to want to branch out and your spouse isn't there yet, that's okay. Be open to what God has for you and prayerfully approach each new opportunity with an open hand. God will bless your efforts to be faithful right where you are far more than when you're trying to force your ideal vision of service onto your spouse or to make it happen in your timing rather than God's.

Keep Walking the Path to Joy

One summer while we were still dating, Josh and I were camp counselors. Each week for eight weeks, we ate three meals a day with a new group of rambunctious preteens and teens, led them through daily camp activities, and kept a watchful eye during "free time." At the ripe old age of twenty, Josh and I felt like we had become parents to ten adolescent girls or boys. Days were filled with activities such as horse riding and canoeing, which many campers were doing for the very first time, and evenings were filled with games, lots of girl talk (for me), hugging those who were homesick, and telling campers that if they didn't get to sleep, they'd be dog-tired the next morning (okay, *I'd* be dog-tired the next morning).

While we both agreed that particular summer was an amazing experience, it was nothing short of *exhausting*. At the end of each week, we had exactly twenty-four hours to go home, shower, sleep, do laundry, and pack up for the start of a new week. On top of this, Josh and I barely saw each other the whole summer. When we applied for the job, I remember thinking how fun it would be to spend the whole summer together. Little did we realize that we were signing up to be sweaty, dirty, and tired, and that we would virtually never see each other until those eight weeks were over.

Marriage can be a lot like that. We go into it expecting one thing but often experience something completely different from what we thought we were signing up for. Maybe we were excited to move on to the next phase in life, to take the next big step in our relationship. Maybe we loved the sense of security and comfort we got from securing our "forever person." Whatever the case, we all go into marriage with certain expectations about what it will provide us—love, happiness, security, status, or approval. Which makes the hard dose of reality most of us receive within those first few years a shocking blow.

That hard dose of reality is finding out your spouse has more flaws than you originally knew about, realizing your selfishness often has a choke hold on your expectations, or simply learning in real time how you both react to and deal with the tough circumstances life throws your way.

On their wedding day, couples promise to walk through these tough life circumstances together without detonating their marriage: "in sickness and in health, for better or for worse." And while many couples can promise to never get divorced, what's much more impressive are the couples who promise to never stop working on their relationship. Couples can agree to stay together for life, but if they never put in the effort to improve themselves and their relationship, they'll be walking out their lifelong commitment on a difficult and painful road.

The couples whose marriages not only last but thrive are those who don't settle for not getting divorced. Instead, they agree to constantly assess the state of their own hearts, make difficult changes, forgive each other, and run to God for his showering of grace, love, and wisdom. It's when couples are mutually willing to lay down their own lives for the sake of displaying the gospel that they not only find the joy that God provides in marriage but also reflect Christ's self-sacrificial and unconditional love for his church to the world around them.

This is God's hope for your marriage—and it's my hope that you are well on your way to that goal. Just as it was for Josh and me the summer we were disillusioned camp counselors, sometimes the work you have to put into your marriage requires much more of you and is much harder than what you thought you had signed up for. It might mean late-night discussions and early-morning prayer and maybe the occasional mid-afternoon breakdown. But as you both seek Christ, you will also find each other along the way. And as you walk that path toward a brighter and more joyful future, you'll discover much more than simply a happy marriage; you'll also discover that through laying down your own lives, you are better equipped to make God's name great through your marriage.

Acknowledgments

I want to thank my literary agent, Kathleen Kerr from Alive Literary Agency, for taking notice of me and my work, coaching me through the writing process, and advocating for me every step of the way. You have been a true friend throughout this process, and I couldn't have made it to the finish line without your help and expertise.

My editors, Christine Anderson and Dirk Buursma, deserve immense thanks for painstakingly polishing my writing to make sure the message I'm so passionate about shines through and is clearly conveyed. Because of you, those who are on a quest to discover God's truth for their marriage will indeed find it. For that, I am forever grateful that you embraced the vision and helped me communicate with clarity and focus.

I am profoundly grateful to the marketing team at Zondervan, who care deeply about the message I want to share about God's purpose for marriage. You have worked diligently to make this book known to anyone and everyone who would need it. Your dedication and enthusiasm have inspired and encouraged me.

Thank you to my husband for unwaveringly and patiently supporting me through the journey of writing this book, especially during a season of transition and life with a newborn. I adore you and am grateful every day for the life and family we work so hard to cultivate. Thank you for walking with me, talking through ideas with me, and being a constant source of love and wisdom in my life.

To Josh's parents, Dave and Camille, and my parents, Lee and Sue—thank you for showing both of us that a marriage can truly thrive when we nurture it, invest in it, and do our very best to love each other as Christ loves his church. We cherish the example you set and the homes we were privileged to grow up in before we met and started a family of our own.

Lastly, I want to thank our church, Grace Church in Greenville, South Carolina, for continuously challenging us, showering us with the truths of the gospel, and placing us in situations where we can serve our local community and be served by our church community. It is an immense blessing to be consistently fed God's truth and to see the gospel lived out daily in and through you.

About Chelsea Damon

Chelsea Damon, an influential blogger and author, has been joyfully married to her husband, Josh, since 2013. Their love story began at Liberty University in Lynchburg, Virginia, where they met during their freshman year. Now residing in South Carolina with their three children and a goofy dog, Chelsea has built a life around fostering healthy, God-centered relationships within marriage and family. Inspired by her own journey, she launched a blog in 2015 dedicated to this mission, followed by the publication of her book *Together with Christ: A Dating Couples Devotional* in 2018.

Chelsea's passion extends beyond just helping Christian couples avoid divorce; she aims to inspire joy, fulfillment, and a deeper purpose within marriage to advance God's kingdom. Outside of writing and speaking on these topics, Chelsea finds joy in gardening with her children, engaging in workouts with her husband, exploring her creative side through painting and writing, and crafting homemade sourdough.